Emotional Intelligence at Work and Beyond

Answer Why EQ, Unlock Self-Awareness, Strengthen Empathy, and Master Communication Skills to Reduce Stress, Build Trust, and Thrive in Every Area of Life

George Munson

GL DIGITAL PUBLISHING LLC

Contents

Introduction

You're standing in the kitchen after a long day. The kids are arguing about something that doesn't matter. Your partner asks you a simple question, but it lands wrong, and suddenly, you snap. Perhaps you regret it immediately, or maybe you walk away, feeling frustrated and unheard. Later, you replay the moment in your mind. "Why did I lose it over something so small?" you wonder. Or it's work: a meeting where you wanted to speak up but froze, or a teammate's offhand comment that left you stewing for hours. If you're like most people, these moments aren't rare; they're part of daily life.

Our world feels like it's rushing forward at double speed. Emails pile up, group chats buzz, and everyone seems to expect instant responses and perfect moods. According to a recent survey, nearly 60% of adults say they feel more stressed and emotionally overwhelmed than ever before. We're more connected and yet, sometimes, more isolated. In this kind of environment, emotional intelligence isn't just a "nice to have." It's a real need. It's what helps us connect, find calm, and get things done without burning out or burning bridges.

So why am I writing this book? My passion for emotional intelligence started with my own struggles, especially in my family and at work. I've seen how communication can fall apart, how misunderstandings can hurt relationships, and how women, in particular, can feel trapped by old patterns and expectations. Over the years, I've talked with hundreds of adults, friends, colleagues, even strangers, about how hard it is to say what you feel, set boundaries, and still feel connected. I want to help, not with lofty ideas, but with real steps anyone can use.

You might be skeptical. You may have tried other self-help books, workshops, or apps. Perhaps you've followed tips on social media or even read about emotional intelligence before, only to feel that nothing has stuck. Maybe you're tired, busy, or discouraged. If that sounds familiar, you're in good company. I'm not here to promise miracles or quick fixes. I get how messy and stubborn emotions can be, and I know how easy it is to lose hope.

However, what makes this book different is that it's about doing, not just reading. Inside, you'll find practical tools, step-by-step scripts, and real-life exercises. Everything is designed for busy adults who want change to show up in real life, not just in theory. Whether you have five minutes or an hour, you'll find something you can use right away. These tools are not just theoretical; they are practical and doable, empowering you to take control of your emotional intelligence.

Each chapter is built around scenarios you actually face, in the office, at family dinners, or over coffee with friends. We'll look at what happens when things go wrong, and we'll break down how to do better next time. You'll get strategies you can try, examples you'll recognize, and troubleshooting tips for when things get tough.

Together, we'll tackle the significant, sticky issues.

- How do you stop yourself from overreacting to a trigger?

- How do you really listen, even when you're annoyed?

- How do you set a boundary without feeling like the "bad guy"?

- How do you break out of old emotional ruts and start fresh?

- How do you build resilience so you bounce back instead of breaking down?

These are the questions real people ask me every day, and they're the questions this book will answer, step by step.

You might be thinking, "But I've tried before and nothing changed." Or, "I'm too busy for this." Or even, "People around me aren't going to change, so what's the point?" I hear you. This book respects your time. The tools here are simple and doable, even if you're juggling a lot. And while I can't promise to change the people around you, I can show you how changing your approach can shift everything, sometimes in ways you don't expect. This book is approachable and understanding, designed to meet you where you are in your journey.

So, what can you expect if you stick with it? You'll start to notice your own patterns. You'll learn how to pause before reacting. You'll find words for feelings you used to bottle up. You'll have new ways to communicate with people you love and those you work with. You'll see old conflicts fade, and new connections grow stronger. You'll move toward your goals, at home, at work, and with friends, more quickly and with less stress. Bit by bit, you'll build a life that feels more open, honest, and rewarding.

Here's how to get the most out of this book: Don't just read, try. Use the scripts. Work through the exercises. Take on the challenges, even the small ones. Keep a journal or jot notes in the margins. Share a new skill with a friend or family member. Every little step counts, and change grows from small, steady actions.

I invite you, regardless of where you're starting from or how many times you've tried before, to join me. Let's move past old barriers, together. Let's build a new set of tools for communication, collaboration, and connection. Whether you're looking for more patience with your kids, a stronger voice at work, or just a little more peace in your daily life, you're in the right place.

So, let's get started. Here's to a journey, one real conversation, one honest feeling, one step at a time, toward the kind of emotional intelligence that actually works, for all of us.

Chapter One

Demystifying Emotional Intelligence for Everyday Life

You're at the dinner table, your child's upset over homework, your partner sighs, and tension fills the air. You want to help, but your response falls flat, and later you wonder why you react the same way every time. These moments are where emotional intelligence, or EQ, becomes invaluable. It's not just a concept for workplace seminars or pop psychology; it's a practical skill set for everyday challenges. With EQ, you can learn to name your feelings, understand others', and keep conversations constructive, even when things get messy. It's a tool that empowers you to navigate family meltdowns and tricky work meetings with confidence and grace.

What Is EQ? Beyond Buzzwords and Into Real Life

In essence, emotional intelligence involves recognizing, understanding, and managing both your own emotions and those of others. It's not about pretending everything is fine or being overly agreeable. Instead, it's about being in tune with what's happening inside you and around you, and choosing thoughtful responses rather than knee-jerk reactions. Suppose IQ measures your ability to solve technical problems or recall information. In that case, EQ gauges your skills in handling emotions and relationships, such as calming yourself before a presentation or reading the mood in a tense meeting.

Practically, imagine two coworkers in a last-minute project crisis. One barks orders; the other takes a breath, acknowledges everyone's stress, then asks for ideas. The latter is using EQ: recognizing their stress, keeping it in check, and helping others do the same. Research shows that while IQ is important for technical issues, EQ is crucial for effective teamwork and building trust. In family life, EQ allows you to avoid pointless arguments and foster honest conversation, helping you manage tantrums or disagreements without yelling or guilt.

EQ is often confused with simply being agreeable or people-pleasing, but there are important distinctions:

EQ vs. Being Nice vs. People-Pleasing

- **Aspect EQ:**

  - Being Nice, People-Pleasing, Core Focus, Understanding & managing emotions, Avoiding conflict.

- **Gaining approval Common Result:**

  - Honest, thoughtful responses, Surface harmony, Self-neglect.

- **Example:**

  - Setting healthy boundaries, speaking up, Always saying yes.

You may have noticed that technical smarts alone don't solve people's problems; brilliant colleagues can still struggle with office politics or emotional confrontations. IQ helps with exams, but EQ enables you to navigate life's more complex aspects.

Consider Sarah, a manager intimidated by giving feedback; her technical knowledge was high, but challenging conversations often went wrong. Once she learned to pause and acknowledge her own discomfort ("This is hard for both of us"), things improved, her team trusted her more, and conversations became less painful.

Or Jamal, a father who tried to "fix" his son's tantrums with lectures. When he started pausing to empathize with his son ("I see this is tough for you") before advising, meltdowns shortened, and their bond improved.

Remember, EQ isn't an innate trait; it's a skill that can be strengthened with practice, feedback, and self-reflection. Think of it like learning a new language, awkward at first, but easier with repetition. This understanding should give you hope and motivation to embark on your EQ journey, knowing that with dedication, you can develop this crucial skill.

The five pillars of EQ:

- **Self-awareness:** Noticing what you're feeling and why, like realizing your heart races when you see a late-night work email.

- **Self-regulation:** Managing your reactions by pausing before firing off an angry reply.

- **Motivation:** Staying committed despite setbacks, pushing through because the goal matters.

- **Empathy:** Sensing others' feelings, catching that "I'm fine" doesn't always mean fine.

- **Social skills:** Navigating conflicts and group dynamics, like smoothing over awkward moments in meetings.

You might picture these pillars as spokes radiating from a hub of self-awareness.

EQ shows up differently at work, at home, and among friends. At work, it's about listening actively and giving effective feedback. At home, it's holding space for your partner's feelings or setting boundaries with relatives. With friends, EQ helps you sense when support or space is needed.

Each area brings unique challenges, work hierarchies, family history, or shifting friendships. If you ever wondered why you freeze up in front of your boss but are short-tempered at home, or why some conflicts linger while others resolve, EQ is likely the root. Throughout this book, you'll find scripts for tricky moments, troubleshooting tips for setbacks, and exercises tailored to different areas of your life, so EQ becomes second nature wherever you go.

Why Emotional Intelligence Matters More Than Ever Today

Swipe, tap, ping - your phone lights up with messages from work, another text from a family member, or a news alert that makes your heart race. These days, it feels like we're always on the go. Digital notifications follow us everywhere, and conversations now occur more often through screens than face-to-face. When tone and body language are absent, misunderstandings appear quickly. You send a short reply on Slack because you're rushing, and suddenly, a teammate thinks you're angry. Or your partner misreads a text as cold or distant, and a tiny spark turns into a full-blown argument. In this rapid-fire world, emotional skills aren't just helpful; they're what keep relationships from unraveling.

Remote work and endless group chats add layers of complexity. At home, the lines blur, family life overlaps with conference calls, and you might find yourself switching between professional and personal roles in a single hour. With so much happening at once, it's easy to misread intentions, take things personally, or snap when stress piles up. The news cycle never stops, bringing fresh waves of uncertainty, and even social media can feel like a minefield for misunderstandings. If you sometimes feel overwhelmed or disconnected, you're not alone.

When emotional intelligence is lacking, the consequences can be severe. Teams struggle to communicate, projects stall because people are afraid to speak up, and high turnover drains energy from the workplace. Studies reveal that employees with low EQ are more likely to leave their jobs, feel disengaged, and contribute to toxic team dynamics. Productivity drops, trust erodes, and everyone pays the price. In families, low EQ often means unresolved conflicts simmer beneath the surface, kids feel unheard, and minor problems spiral out of control. Friendships can wither when someone doesn't pick up on subtle signals or pushes boundaries without realizing.

A recent workplace survey found that over 70% of employees believe emotional intelligence is more important for team success than technical skills alone. Low EQ makes tough conversations harder and feedback feel personal, even when it's not meant that way. I've watched simple miscommunications escalate into team drama simply because someone misunderstood an email's tone or failed to check in when a colleague appeared stressed.

You might recognize the fallout from low EQ in your own life. Maybe you've experienced a meeting where no one listened, voices rose, and nothing got decided except who felt bruised afterward. Or a minor disagreement at home snowballed into days of tension. These aren't rare accidents; they're regular outcomes when emotional awareness takes a backseat.

The opposite is also true. Research consistently shows that emotional intelligence predicts better outcomes at work and at home. People with higher EQ handle change with more ease and recover faster from setbacks. They communicate more clearly and adapt when plans shift. Relationships last longer because both sides feel seen and respected. Teams led by emotionally intelligent managers are more productive and have lower turnover; everyone feels safer sharing ideas, taking risks, and supporting one another.

EQ isn't just about business success or job titles; it's about living with less stress and a deeper connection. Consider your own goals; you want to navigate tough talks without feeling defensive or help your kids open up instead of shutting down. You're aiming for smoother teamwork at the office or hoping to have fewer misunderstandings with friends. Emotional intelligence is the tool that moves you from reacting out of habit to responding with purpose.

Suppose you crave more honest conversations, fewer regretful outbursts, or simply a sense of calm in the chaos of modern life. In that case, EQ is the skill set that makes those changes possible. It bridges gaps between generations at home and brings clarity to complicated group projects at work. You don't need to be perfect to benefit, just be willing to pay attention to feelings (yours and others'), try new strategies, and pick yourself up when things go sideways.

This book is built for these times: fast-paced, unpredictable, sometimes overwhelming. The tools here are designed for people who want more than theory; they want real change, and they can see it in their daily routines. Whether you're sending texts from your kitchen table or leading a Zoom call full of muted faces, emotional intelligence is the bridge between what you hope for and what actually happens in your conversations and relationships.

Busting the "Born This Way" Myth: EQ Is Learnable

It's easy to believe that some people are just "naturals" when it comes to emotions. Maybe you've told yourself, "I'm just not good at this stuff," or heard a friend say, "She's always been sensitive, me, not so much." This is one of the biggest myths holding people back from real progress. Emotional intelligence isn't a fixed trait like eye color. It's a collection of skills that can be strengthened, fine-tuned, and expanded at any age. Think about learning to ride a bike or picking up a new language as an adult; the first attempts feel awkward and clumsy, but over time, with practice, things click. The same applies to EQ. Science backs this up: our brains are wired for change. Neuroplasticity, the brain's way of forming new connections, means you can actually rewire emotional habits through repeated, intentional action. Studies show adults have improved their emotional intelligence through targeted practice, sometimes in just a few months. Even if you've always reacted the same way in arguments or found it challenging to understand others, you're not stuck.

Let me share two stories that illustrate this idea. The first involves a colleague who was once notorious for shutting down during conflict. Meetings would heat up, her face would go blank, and she'd retreat into silence. She worried she'd never be able to speak up or manage her anxiety in those moments. Instead of giving up, she started with tiny experiments, writing down her feelings before meetings, practicing simple breathing techniques, and using one sentence to express herself during tense conversations. At first, she stumbled, but after a few months, not only did she start contributing more, but her team began to seek her input during tough decisions. Her newfound confidence was evident, and people took notice.

The second story comes from home life. A father I know struggled for years with patience. After long workdays, his kids' chaos left him frazzled, and he'd snap or walk away to avoid saying something he'd regret. He decided to try small changes: pausing for three deep breaths when frustration rose, and using simple phrases like "I need a minute" instead of yelling. It wasn't magic; sometimes, he still lost his cool, but slowly, he noticed fewer blowups and more moments where his kids actually listened to him. These shifts didn't happen because he suddenly became a different person; they happened because he practiced new habits until they stuck.

Setbacks are part of the process. No one gets it right every time, not me, not you, not anyone who's ever tried to change how they handle emotions. If you've tried before and slipped back into old habits, it doesn't mean you're hopeless or incapable. Growth is awkward and sometimes frustrating.

That's normal. The important thing is to expect imperfection and keep trying different approaches until you find what works for you.

What sets this book apart is its focus on these everyday micro-habits, tiny actions you can repeat often without needing hours of free time or superhuman discipline. You'll see exercises that fit into the cracks of your real life: jotting down three emotions each morning, using a favorite phrase to cool off during an argument, or reflecting for sixty seconds after a tough interaction. Repetition is the secret sauce here; the more you practice these small skills, the more automatic they feel.

Each chapter will provide you with practical tools to use in honest conversations and real-life situations. These are not just theoretical concepts that sound good on paper but fall apart when your boss is annoyed or your family is loud and tired. You won't find pressure to be perfect or "fix" yourself overnight; instead, you'll get strategies that help you notice progress one conversation, one boundary, one breath at a time. If you're willing to try, even imperfectly, your brain can adapt and your relationships can shift. EQ is something you build, not something you're born with or forever without.

A Practical Overview of the Five Pillars of EQ

Think of emotional intelligence as a sturdy house with five strong pillars holding up the roof. Each pillar supports daily life in its own way, and together, they keep things steady even during emotional storms. Suppose you're looking to understand how to put EQ into practice. In that case, it helps to know these five core components: self-awareness, self-regulation, motivation, empathy, and social skills. Each one is simple to define, yet powerful when put to use.

Self-awareness is the ability to notice and understand what you feel, as you think it. It's that split-second when your chest tightens before a big conversation or your mood shifts after reading a stressful email. You catch yourself thinking, "Wow, I'm really anxious right now." At work, this shows up before you share an idea in a meeting, you sense your nerves and acknowledge them instead of ignoring them. At home, you may notice your irritation rising when your sibling brings up that same old topic at family dinner. With friends, it could be realizing you feel left out when plans are made without you. This awareness is the first step toward choosing your response, instead of getting swept away by old habits.

Self-regulation follows closely behind. This is the skill that helps you manage how you express your emotions, so your feelings don't control your actions. Imagine reading an email that instantly pushes your buttons. Your first impulse might be to fire off a snarky reply. Self-regulation means pausing for a breath, letting the initial wave of frustration pass, and then choosing words that won't make things worse. In family life, picture yourself biting your tongue instead of snapping at your partner after a long day. Among friends, it might be holding back from gossiping when you're annoyed. Self-regulation isn't about hiding what you feel; it's about expressing it in a way that doesn't hurt you or others.

Motivation is your inner drive, the force that keeps you going even when things get tough. It's what helps you stick with a project at work despite obstacles or setbacks. Maybe you're working late because you care about the outcome, not just because someone told you to finish the task. At home, motivation helps you stay present with your kids or partner, even after a draining week. Socially, it enables you to show up for friends' important events or reach out to mend a rift after an argument. Motivation in EQ means acting from purpose and meaning, not just obligation or reward.

Empathy is the capacity to sense and understand what others are feeling, even if they don't say it directly. It goes beyond "being nice" and involves really tuning in to another person's emotional state. When a friend insists they're "fine," empathy helps you pick up on the sadness in their voice or the tension in their posture. At work, this means noticing when a colleague is unusually quiet in a meeting and checking in. In family life, empathy appears when you recognize your child's frustration over homework or understand your partner's stress without them having to spell it out. Empathy fosters trust and makes others feel valued and seen.

Social skills are the set of abilities that help you navigate interactions with others, resolve conflicts, build connections, persuade when needed, or smooth over rough patches. Think about the last time you accidentally offended a colleague; social skills help you apologize sincerely and repair the relationship. At home, it could be finding the right words to resolve an argument without keeping score. With friends, it could include someone new in your circle or de-escalating tension during a heated group debate. Social skills make teamwork easier and help relationships grow stronger.

The EQ Pillars Visual

If this book had a visual model, and I recommend keeping one handy as you read, it would be a pentagon with each pillar (self-awareness, self-regulation, motivation, empathy, social skills) at a corner and "emotional intelligence" written boldly in the center. Whenever you face an emotional challenge, glance at this mental diagram and ask yourself which pillar might help most right now.

Each of these five pillars will get its own spotlight later in the book. There will be sections packed with practical tools, scripts for tricky conversations, exercises to build each skill, and real examples from work, family, and social circles. We'll examine how small changes in each pillar can lead to significant shifts in everyday life. If you've ever wished for a set of instructions for handling emotions, your own or someone else's, these pillars are your starting point.

How EQ Shows Up Differently at Work, Home, and With Friends

Emotional intelligence (EQ) doesn't present itself the same way in every environment. Moving from the office to home and out with friends, EQ skills shift, sometimes subtly, sometimes sharply. At work, EQ means maintaining composure when meetings unravel or when a colleague complains. You listen, reflect, and respond thoughtfully, striking a balance between honesty and kindness when giving feedback, thereby avoiding damage to trust. When a boss assigns a last-minute project, your initial reaction might be stress or frustration, but with EQ, you pause, regulate your emotions, and seek clarity instead. These moments, reading the room, managing yourself, and adapting quickly, are all EQ in action.

Work's power dynamics add complexity: impressing managers, getting along with peers, and navigating tricky personalities without losing your cool. "Managing up" requires you to support your supervisor without appearing overbearing, demonstrating initiative without arrogance, and pushing back respectfully. When EQ falters, misunderstandings and grudges linger, and minor issues can become central tension. Yet, using EQ at work boosts not only your relationships but also your reputation as a calm, solutions-focused team member.

Home brings a different emotional climate. Here, EQ centers on safety, comfort, and genuine honesty. Holding space for a partner is often about listening without immediately fixing or judging. If your spouse vents about a tough day, EQ means validating their feelings, "That sounds exhausting", instead of jumping to solutions or getting defensive. Extended family and in-laws often test boundaries; saying "no" when tradition or guilt weighs in can be hard, so you need to balance honesty with care to avoid unnecessary conflict.

Generational differences come to the fore at home. Parents and children often differ in how emotions "should" be shown. One might want to talk things out, another needs alone time. Old family patterns can resurface quickly; suddenly, you find yourself reacting as your teenage self instead of as an adult. EQ breaks these cycles by making room for differing needs and encouraging open, honest (not just polite) communication.

With friends, EQ looks different again. Even casual get-togethers can harbor undercurrents of tension or miscommunication. You might sense friction at a party, a glance or posture gives something away. EQ here means adjusting your own approach, changing the topic, or checking in quietly with someone who seems off.

When friends vent about stress or struggles, they typically want empathy, not advice. Responding well means validating their feelings, "That sounds rough; I'm here if you want to talk", not jumping to quick fixes. Group dynamics can add complexity: sometimes you mediate, sometimes you need support, but feel awkward asking.

Why are these settings so different? At work, interactions center around reputation, career, and collaboration. At home, deeper connections and old issues often color your responses. With friends, it's balancing trust with keeping things fun and easy. Each domain has its own trouble spots: freezing in work tension but snapping at home, being open with friends but guarded with family, or finding it easier to draw boundaries at work than with relatives.

People often wonder, "Why can I handle my boss's criticism but lose patience with my partner?" or "Why am I honest with friends but clam up with my parents?" Context matters. Your emotional intelligence responds to surroundings; what's right in one space may not work in another.

That's why this book avoids generic advice. Instead, you'll find tailored scripts for tricky work conversations, exercises for handling family triggers, and practical tips for social awkwardness. Each tool helps you build EQ exactly where you need it, at work, at home, or with friends.

As you continue, remember that emotional intelligence isn't just something you possess; it's a skill you adapt to each specific setting. This flexibility is what makes EQ such a powerful and practical tool for every aspect of life.

Chapter Two

Building Self-Awareness That Sticks

A Step-by-Step Guide to Spotting Your Emotional Triggers

Have you ever experienced a sudden shift in your mood, such as when you're interrupted in a conversation or when a coworker's response to your well-thought-out email is a single word, 'Noted'? Perhaps it's a partner's raised voice or a knot in your stomach upon seeing a particular text. These are emotional triggers, and they're a standard part of the human experience. Triggers are not a sign of weakness or oversensitivity; they're your brain's way of alerting you to potential threats, whether it's criticism, disrespect, or feeling ignored. Everyone has them. Some people freeze, others become defensive, and some withdraw. It's all normal, and the more you acknowledge them, the less power they have over you.

Emotional triggers are like invisible tripwires. Small things, a curt message from your boss at night, laughter at your idea in a meeting, or a song recalling tough memories, can set them off. Often, the reaction seems excessive, but it's real for you because triggers often link to old experiences or core beliefs ("I'm not good enough," "People don't respect me"). Over time, these become patterns —your default emotional shortcuts when you're stressed.

Start by identifying your triggers as they happen. Notice physical signs: chest tightening, clenched jaw, flushed face, racing pulse, gut discomfort, restless hands, or a need to leave the room. These cues are your "check engine light." When they appear, pause and note: What happened? Who was there? What words or actions set this off?

For the next three days, keep a "trigger log." Use a notebook or your phone's notes app. Whenever an emotion flares up (such as annoyance, embarrassment, anger, or defensiveness), jot down what happened just before. Who was present? Was it work, home, or text? Note your body's reaction and your immediate response, even if you just wanted to roll your eyes or retreat to the bathroom. The goal isn't self-judgment; it's data collection, like a scientist studying yourself.

After a few days, review your log. Patterns typically emerge. Maybe your sibling's comments on your career make you feel judged and defensive, or Monday mornings bring anxiety due to team check-ins. Social situations might trigger feelings of being invisible if friends exclude you, or irritation when interrupted. At work, public feedback could make you want to shrink. At home, criticism from a parent might set off old defensive reactions. These patterns highlight where your self-awareness needs focus.

Trigger Tracker Worksheet

Use this for at least three days to track your emotional responses:

- **Situation:** What happened? Where? Who was there?

- **Trigger:** Which words/actions/sounds were the spark?

- **Physical Signs:** What did you notice in your body (tense jaw, racing heart, nausea)?

- **Emotion:** What emotion surfaced (anger, shame, sadness)?

- **Initial Reaction:** What did you do (snapped, went silent, left the room)?

After three days, review your notes. Are certain people recurring? Are there topics or locations that always trigger you (office kitchen, family group chats)? The aim isn't to avoid these situations but to recognize them so you're not blindsided.

Knowing your triggers isn't about blaming others for your reactions; it's about reclaiming control over your responses. The more precise you are on which situations trigger you, the more tools you have for responding differently next time. And everyone's list is unique; what unsettles you might not bother someone else at all. Appreciate every "aha" moment, even if it's just noticing you tense up or hating specific phrases like "Calm down" or "You're overreacting."

As your awareness grows, you may notice new patterns. Triggers aren't always big blowups; sometimes they're minor irritations that add up, such as feeling rushed during morning routines or being ignored in work emails. These details are clues that help you tune in before emotions take over.

Ultimately, the goal of identifying triggers is not to avoid all emotional reactions. It's about gaining a moment's pause, a chance to choose your response, instead of letting triggers dictate it. This pause is where real self-awareness begins: recognizing what sets you off and taking ownership of your reactions. By doing so, you empower yourself to manage your emotional responses more effectively.

The "Emotional Audit": A Five-Minute Daily Check-In

Building real self-awareness is not about having one big realization and calling it a day. It's all about little moments where you pause, check in with yourself, and actually notice what's going on inside. That's where the "emotional audit" comes in. This habit isn't complicated or time-consuming, but it does ask you to be more intentional with your feelings, even if it's for a few minutes. Here's how it works: pick a time, right before breakfast, after you park your car, or during a quiet moment in the evening. Set a timer on your phone for five minutes. Now, ask yourself three questions. What am I feeling right now? Why do I think I'm feeling this way? What do I need at this moment? You don't need fancy language or perfect grammar. Just jot down whatever pops up, such as "I'm restless because I have a tight deadline" or "I feel irritated but not sure why, maybe just tired." Sometimes the answer is clear, other times it's foggy. The point isn't to analyze every detail but to be honest with yourself for a few minutes.

Doing an emotional audit every day might sound like overkill, but the truth is, consistency is where the magic happens. Consider brushing your teeth: one time won't make much of a difference, but doing it daily helps keep things healthy. The same goes for emotional check-ins. When you make this a regular part of your day, even if you only manage four days out of seven, you'll start to spot trends in your mood and reactions that you used to miss. Some days, nothing major comes up. On other days, you might realize you're on edge all morning because of an awkward conversation from the night before. The more you practice, the easier it gets to recognize subtle shifts and name them without judgment. Over weeks, this routine quietly rewires how you relate to your own feelings.

Now, life doesn't always allow for five uninterrupted minutes of reflection, especially when work or family chaos takes over. If that's your reality, try the "micro-audit." This is a one-minute pause, sometimes just thirty seconds, where you use a sticky note or set a reminder on your phone: "How am I feeling right now?" Please keep it simple. Glance at your message midmorning, on the subway, or in the middle of errands. Even a quick scan, "Tired and tense, need coffee," or "Surprisingly calm for a Monday", counts as progress. These micro-audits can be surprisingly eye-opening. Done regularly, they still build muscle memory for self-awareness.

Of course, sticking with any habit has its hurdles. Some days you'll forget. Other times, you might feel silly or uncomfortable, especially if talking about emotions isn't your usual thing. Words don't come easily, or you draw a blank. That's normal. When this happens, start with basic feeling categories: mad, sad, glad, or afraid. If nothing fits perfectly, pick the closest word and move on. Over time, naming gets easier and more precise as you practice. If discomfort about naming feelings persists, remind yourself that this is a private matter; no one else sees your notes unless you choose to share them.

Another common barrier is doubting whether these check-ins really matter. It's easy to think, "How will stopping for a minute change anything?" But just like tracking expenses helps with saving money or logging meals brings awareness to eating habits, emotional audits reveal patterns you'd otherwise overlook. Sometimes you'll notice that certain days are always more stressful or that your mood dips after specific meetings or activities. Once you see these patterns clearly on paper (or screen), you can respond with more intention instead of just reacting blindly.

If writing things down feels awkward at first, try speaking your answers into your phone's voice notes or using an app designed for quick reflections. Some people prefer typing in a running document or even texting themselves as a way to capture what's going on. The format doesn't matter; what matters is building a habit that works for your life and feels natural enough to keep up.

There will be times when your emotional audit uncovers things you'd rather not face, resentment toward a coworker, sadness about an old argument, or guilt over snapping at someone close. That's part of the process as well. Simply noticing these emotions without rushing to fix them is a huge step forward. It gives you more space between what happens and how you respond.

If you're someone who likes visual reminders, use symbols or simple doodles next to each emotion: a cloud for confusion, a sun for contentment, lightning for anger. These little cues can make the process less intimidating and more personal.

The goal isn't perfection; it's progress through regular attention and tiny steps forward. The five-minute daily check-in becomes a gentle anchor point, a way to reconnect with yourself no matter how busy things get or how many hats you're wearing each day.

Naming Your Feelings Accurately And Why It Matters

For many, naming feelings doesn't come naturally. You might think, "I'm upset," or "I feel off," and stop there. But there's real science showing why describing your emotions more precisely, like "I'm disappointed because I was left out" instead of just "I'm sad", actually calms your brain. Using words for emotions moves your brain activity from the survival center to areas where you can think more clearly. You become less overwhelmed and more able to choose your response, even if the situation hasn't changed. It's biology, not magic: labeling helps you step back, observe, and act instead of being flooded by feeling.

Emotional illiteracy is common; if you find it tricky to name your feelings beyond "angry," "sad," or "fine," you're not alone. Many people grew up where big emotions weren't discussed, or only a few emotions were "allowed," hearing things like "boys don't cry" or "don't make a scene." Over time, this narrows your emotional vocabulary, so you might mix up irritation and anger or mistake anxiety for excitement. The good news is you can expand your emotional vocabulary just like learning any new language: the more words you know, the better you understand what's happening inside you.

Most stick to basic feelings: mad, sad, glad, afraid. But life is more nuanced. Emotions can be tangled and fleeting. Here are some less common, but essential, feeling words:

- **Resentful** – a mix of anger and unfairness

- **Overlooked** – feeling ignored

- **Restless** – uneasy, unsure why

- **Hopeful** - anticipating something positive

- **Anxious** – nervous about the future

- **Ashamed** – embarrassed by what you did/are

- **Content** – peacefully satisfied

- **Grateful** – deep appreciation

- **Disappointed** let down by unmet expectations

- **Vulnerable** – emotionally/physically exposed

- **Jealousy** – wanting what others have

- **Relieved** – stress lifted

- **Irritated** – minor annoyance

- **Lonely** – isolated or disconnected

- **Motivated** – energized for action

- **Stressed** under pressure

- **Defensive** – protecting from criticism

- **Confused** – uncertain

- **Inspired** – sudden creativity or motivation

Learning words like these helps you get specific. Instead of just "bad," you might realize you feel overlooked at work and restless at home, which is more actionable and easier to address.

For a visual tool, use the "feelings wheel" (https://feelingswheel.com/). This wheel begins with core feelings, such as happy, sad, angry, and scared, and then expands to more nuanced emotions. It's practical for daily life, not just therapy: when words don't come, glance at the wheel to see what resonates with you. Sometimes, the right word shifts your perspective.

To practice, try this exercise: keep a feelings journal for a week. Each day, at three different times (morning, midday, evening), write exactly what you're feeling using one of these more nuanced words. Don't settle for broad terms like "bad" or "fine." Get specific: is it irritation from being interrupted again, disappointment from canceled plans, or relief after finishing a challenging project? Add context if you can: "I felt envious when my coworker got praise," or "hopeful after the team agreed on my idea." This isn't about judging yourself, it's about getting clear.

You may be surprised how often your emotions shift or how naming them makes them easier to manage. Over time, you'll be able to communicate your needs more clearly at work, at home, and with friends. Instead of snapping at your partner or withdrawing at work, you'll be able to say, "I'm feeling overlooked," or "I'm anxious about tomorrow's meeting," which opens the door for support and better problem-solving.

To go further, challenge yourself to learn two new feeling words each week and spot them in your life. The more precise your language, the more agency you gain over your emotions. Emotional literacy isn't just a fancy skill; it smooths life, clarifies communication, and makes relationships less rocky.

Unpacking Repetitive Emotional Patterns to Explain Why You Feel Stuck

If life feels like you're stuck in a loop, repeating the same arguments, frustrations, and outcomes, it's not a sign of laziness or failure. Instead, your brain craves the familiar, even if that means staying in cycles of emotional chaos. These loops are ingrained, much like ruts on a well-traveled dirt road. Think about the last time you argued with a loved one: the details may differ, but the underlying script plays out in a familiar pattern, tension escalates, voices rise, someone withdraws or leaves, and guilt or regret follows. The cycle then quietly waits to start anew. This experience is common and entirely human.

You can demystify these emotional cycles by mapping them. Select one relationship or situation that feels repetitive, such as with your partner, boss, or child. Reflect on what triggers the cycle. For example, every time your spouse mentions spending, you may instantly bristle and respond sharply, leading to hours of cold silence. Or, in meetings, you might freeze when asked for input, then later berate yourself for staying quiet, making you less likely to speak up next time. Write down what happens before, during, and after these incidents, including inner thoughts and feelings, not just external words or actions.

Focus on the sequence: most patterns begin with a single spark, a comment, a look, or even an unspoken assumption. This triggers an emotion (anger, shame, anxiety) that leads to a habitual reaction (lashing out, shutting down, avoidance). The aftermath is often marked by simmering resentment or lingering guilt. Through this process, you'll see how automatic these responses are.

These emotional loops don't arise to torment you; they often serve as protection or signal unmet needs. Defensiveness at work might come from fear of being seen as incompetent. Snapping at coworkers may be an attempt to cover insecurity. With family, withdrawing during arguments might be tied to old feelings of powerlessness or being unheard. If these patterns show up in many areas of your life, ask yourself what underlying needs aren't being met. Is there a longing for respect, safety, or unresolved wounds? Although such reflection can be uncomfortable, it's invaluable.

Breaking these cycles doesn't require a dramatic transformation. Start with a "pattern interrupt", a deliberate pause in your routine reaction. If you sense your familiar emotional loop beginning (anger, anxiety, defensiveness), acknowledge it mentally: "This is my old pattern. What can

22

I do differently?" That brief moment of awareness is decisive; it allows you to step back and choose a new response. You might ask a question instead of snapping back or take a walk before responding to an irritating email.

Consider Jamie, a manager who dreads feedback sessions because she gets defensive and makes excuses. Once she maps her cycle (anticipation > tension > defensiveness > regret), she decides to ask for a moment before responding. The next time tension rises, she says, "Give me a second to think about that," instead of immediately justifying herself. It doesn't fix everything instantly, but it slows the pattern and gives her space for new choices.

Or Alex, a parent whose arguments with his teenager repeatedly end with him shutting down and retreating to his phone, leaving the issue unresolved. His intervention is to name the pattern as it starts: "I notice I'm shutting down." Saying this out loud sometimes shifts the energy, helping him stay present or return more quickly.

Then there's Priya, who feels anxious about asking questions at her fast-paced job. Her pattern is anxiety-avoidance-guilt: fear makes her stay silent, then she feels guilty for missing information. Priya's intervention is to write out one question before each meeting and commit to asking it at least once weekly. These small changes help break the loop.

You won't disrupt the cycle perfectly every time. Even just noticing the pattern and naming it helps weaken its hold. With practice, the old ruts become shallower and easier to step out of. Every pause is evidence that change is possible, you're learning to reshape your responses and write a new script, moment by moment.

From Overwhelm to Clarity by Using Mood Trackers and Micro-Reflections

Building self-awareness doesn't need to be overwhelming or just another chore. One of the simplest ways to gain insight into your emotional life is by tracking your moods. This involves more than just labeling a day as "good" or "bad." Think of mood tracking as shining a light into the less visible parts of your emotions, revealing patterns you might otherwise miss. You can do this using a notebook, planner, computer, or simply your phone's notes app. Each evening, rate your mood on a scale from 1 to 10, 1 meaning "totally exhausted or upset" and 10 for "on top of the world." Next to your score, jot a few notes about standout events, a tense meeting, a funny moment, an argument, or just a walk that helped you reset.

Some people find writing things down on paper to be most helpful, while others prefer the convenience of an app. If tech is your thing, apps like *Moodnotes* and *Daylio* offer easy ways to log your mood quickly, often with reminders and colorful charts. *Moodnotes* focuses on thought patterns, while *Daylio* makes tracking simple with icons and short notes. Other options, such as *Moodfit* or the "*How We Feel*" app, offer more features while remaining user-friendly. Whether you use a journal or an app, the goal remains the same: capture what's really happening in your mood, so you can spot real trends.

Pairing mood tracking with micro-reflections can amplify your self-awareness. After rating your mood, take thirty seconds to answer two questions: What went well today? What felt demanding or draining? No need for lengthy entries; simply note the first thing that comes to mind ("Great lunch with a friend," or "Felt anxious before a meeting"). This isn't about digging for drama, but about getting in the habit of noticing both the positives and the tough spots. Over time, these brief reflections create a personal emotional map, highlighting where you thrive and what tends to sap your energy.

After a few weeks, patterns start to appear, maybe Mondays feel tougher, Fridays lighter, or stress spikes before certain recurring events. Do you notice that arguments occur more frequently on certain days? Does a particular project sap your mood? Trends like these are valuable. They offer concrete evidence rather than vague feelings of being "off." With this clarity, you can schedule more breaks, prepare differently for meetings, or make other minor tweaks that ease your week.

Tracking doesn't have to focus only on the negatives. Noting your successes is just as important; maybe you handled a challenging situation better than before or noticed you bounced back faster from stress. Celebrate catching yourself before snapping or choosing a healthy outlet for frustration. These small victories matter. Acknowledging progress keeps your motivation alive and shifts self-awareness from something critical to something encouraging.

If you ever feel stuck, like nothing's improving, review your past entries. Sometimes growth is subtle, such as recovering from setbacks more quickly or having shorter arguments. Give yourself credit for consistently showing up and paying attention. There's no need for perfection; noticing your emotional world is a form of progress in itself.

Mood tracking takes less than five minutes a day once you're used to it. The key is building it into your routine, while waiting in line, unwinding at night, or first thing in the morning. Skipping a day here and there is fine; what matters is showing up often enough to spot patterns in how you feel and how you relate to others.

To wrap up: self-awareness isn't about becoming someone new overnight. It's about noticing what's real for you and finding clarity in daily life. Regular mood tracking and quick reflections provide a strong foundation for what's next, learning how to stay calm and respond thoughtfully when emotions run high. In the next chapter, we'll look at practical ways to keep your cool under pressure and manage emotions during stressful moments.

Chapter Three

Mastering Self-Regulation by Staying Calm Under Pressure

The Mindful Pause, or, How to Respond Instead of React

You know that feeling when your heart races after a snide comment or "here we go again" flashes in your mind before a group text erupts? Life tosses fastballs our way with little warning, sending adrenaline surging, muscles tensing, and your mind spinning with frustration, embarrassment, or anger. In those moments, it's easy to act on instinct, snapping back, raising your voice, or shutting down. This loop can feel automatic, but you can break it. The mindful pause is your tool for doing just that, giving you a chance to choose a better response.

A mindful pause is a brief, conscious space between a trigger and your reaction. It's not about ignoring or suppressing your feelings; it's about noticing what's happening, breathing, and deciding your response. When you're triggered, your brain's amygdala sounds the alarm, and fight, flight, or freeze kicks in before you can think. The pause, even for a few seconds, allows your prefrontal cortex, responsible for reasoning, to take charge, enabling you to act intentionally. This simple shift puts you back in control.

Here's how to practice the mindful pause: First, notice the urge to react. Catching yourself is half the battle, since reactions are so quick. It might be heat in your cheeks, a knot in your stomach, or the urge to fire off a reply. That's your cue. Next, take three slow, deliberate breaths. Focus on your breath to calm your system and give yourself a few extra seconds. As you breathe, quietly name what you're feeling: "annoyed," "anxious," "hurt." Don't judge, name it. Finally, choose your response with intention instead of falling back on knee-jerk habits. Ask: "What outcome do I want? What's my best move?" Then respond deliberately.

Let's look at real-life examples. At work, you get a snarky email from a colleague. Instinct tells you to fire back, but you pause. After three breaths, you label your feelings ("I feel disrespected"), then draft a reply but wait ten minutes before sending. When you reread it, you soften the tone, sticking to facts to keep things productive.

Imagine you're at a grocery store. Your child whines loudly for candy; embarrassment flares as people glare. Instead of snapping or giving in, you pause, breathe, and name your feelings ("frustrated and embarrassed"). Then you respond calmly: "I see you want candy. We're not buying it today," steering the moment without threats or bribes.

Or, it's a group text spiraling into a heated debate. You feel dismissed when your suggestion is ignored. Rather than shooting back or leaving the chat, you put down your phone and breathe three times, admit to yourself ("I feel dismissed"), then choose to express your desire to be included, preventing resentment or argument.

Try Your Own Mindful Pause

Write these steps on a sticky note:

- Notice the urge

- Take three slow breaths

- Name the feeling

- Choose your response

Put it somewhere you'll see often. For the next three days, pick a situation each day, big or small, where you practice these steps. Jot down what happened and how you felt afterward.

If you forget to pause, that's normal, especially with high emotions. Start with low-stakes situations like slow drivers, minor work annoyances, or daily family routines. It might feel awkward or pointless at first, but repeated practice builds a habit. If you slip up, reflect later, "How could I have paused?", and try again next time. Over time, pausing becomes second nature, helping you stay steady when life gets loud.

Scripts That Really Work to Tame Defensiveness in Criticism

Defensiveness is a natural response to criticism, especially if you care about doing well. Your brain wants to protect you, so any form of feedback can feel threatening. The urge to explain, deflect, or withdraw isn't a flaw; it's your mind and body trying to keep you safe, a reaction shaped early on by teachers, parents, or bosses who focused more on mistakes than successes. No wonder phrases like "Can I give you some feedback?" make you brace yourself.

Psychologically, defensiveness is straightforward. Criticism triggers your brain's alarm system (the amygdala), flooding you with stress and thoughts like, "It's not fair," "You don't get my side," or "I'm going to get blamed." You might lash out or shut down, both of which are common, though neither helps you grow or solve anything. The good news: staying open to feedback is a skill you can learn. You can train yourself to pause, reset, and respond thoughtfully.

Here's a three-step script that works in the moment, without faking calm you don't feel. First, acknowledge you've heard the feedback ("Thank you for sharing"). This slows things down and shows respect for the other person's effort. Next, claim a moment to think: "Let me consider that for a moment before I respond." This gives your brain time to process, instead of reacting defensively. Finally, invite more information if unclear or emotions are high: "I hear you, and I'd like to better understand your perspective." This signals your willingness to listen, not just defend.

These scripts aren't magic, but they shift the energy in difficult conversations. For example, at work: "When I hear your feedback on my recent project, my first reaction is to feel overwhelmed. Let me pause before I respond." At home: "When I hear you feel unsupported, my first reaction is guilt and wanting to argue. I need a second to take this in." With friends: "When I hear you're frustrated with our plans, my first reaction is defensiveness. I want to understand where you're coming from."

Fill-in-the-blank templates help in the heat of the moment:

- "When I hear _____, my first reaction is _____. Let me check in with myself before I respond."

- "Thank you for telling me _____. I'm processing how that feels."

- "Hearing _____ brings up _____ for me. Can we talk about what would help us move forward?"

These phrases help you move from a defensive reaction toward genuine dialogue, and encourage healthier communication patterns for those around you, family, coworkers, even kids, showing it's okay to pause before replying.

What if things get heated anyway? Sometimes emotions rise, no matter how hard you try to remain calm. You might shut down, or the conversation might spiral. It's entirely valid to pause and say, "I'm starting to feel overwhelmed, I need a break." This isn't avoidance, but a way to prevent things from escalating. You can take a short walk or agree to resume later when everyone's calmer. If someone pushes back when you ask for space, calmly repeat: "I want this to go well, so I need a few minutes."

The goal isn't to never feel defensive, you're human, but to recognize when you are and use these scripts to get unstuck. Over time, these approaches make feedback less distressing. You'll spend less time stewing over criticism and more time actually listening, even if it stings.

Even after using these scripts, your body may still react; you might shake or your heart might race. Remind yourself that this feeling is temporary and doesn't define your worth. If needed, jot down what happened, what was said, how you felt, what helped or didn't, to use as practice and reflection for next time.

Learning new responses takes patience. You may slip into old habits when stressed or tired, but each attempt is progress. As these scripts become second nature, staying open and even curious when faced with criticism gets easier.

Calming Panic Fast: Micro-Habits for Stressful Work Moments

Work has a way of throwing curveballs that hit you right in the gut. Maybe you're halfway through your coffee when your manager pings you for an impromptu meeting. Or you're called on to present with zero warning, and your mind goes blank. That creeping dread before a performance review, the tightness in your chest during a heated team call, or the rush of nerves as you skim through last-minute feedback, all of these moments provoke panic, even in the most seasoned professionals. Sometimes it's subtle: sweaty palms, a racing heart, or a blank mind when you need your words the most. Other times, it's more obvious, a full-blown urge to run out of the meeting room, hide in the bathroom, or shut your laptop and pretend none of it is happening.

Those reactions are normal. They're your brain's way of sounding the alarm when things feel unpredictable or out of control. But you don't have to get swept away by them. Quick, on-the-spot micro-habits can help you regain a sense of control, even when the pressure is on and you feel like you're about to unravel. These are little tools, practices that take less than two minutes, that you can use without anyone noticing. They're like emotional first aid kits for your workday.

One of the easiest, and surprisingly effective, tools is the "4-7-8" breathing exercise. Here's how it works: breathe in quietly through your nose for a count of four, hold that breath for seven seconds (as best as you can), then exhale slowly through your mouth for eight seconds. You might want to do this with your hands under your desk, your feet flat on the floor, and your eyes down at your notebook, so no one suspects a thing. This kind of deep, intentional breathing helps slow your heart rate and signals your brain that you're not actually in danger, even if it feels that way. It only takes two or three rounds before things start to shift inside you.

Grounding with your five senses is another excellent way to get out of your head and back into the present. When panic hits, your mind races through all kinds of worst-case scenarios, losing your train of thought, embarrassing yourself, and forgetting what you meant to say. To interrupt that spiral, look around and mentally list five things you can see (the color of a coworker's shirt, a stapler, the pattern on the carpet), four things you can touch (the smoothness of your pen, the texture of your sweater), three things you hear (keyboards tapping, a distant conversation), two things you smell (coffee, perfume), and one thing you taste (gum, breath mint). Anchoring yourself in these sensory details pulls you back from panic. It helps you focus on what's actually happening, not what might go wrong.

If you need something even more subtle, try a mini body scan while sitting at your desk. Start at your toes and move up: notice if they're tense or relaxed, then move to your calves, knees, thighs, up to your shoulders and neck. As you scan each area, release any tension you find, wiggle your toes inside your shoes, or roll your shoulders back a bit. No one needs to see what you're doing; it's all about quietly tuning in and releasing stress bit by bit.

Self-talk is powerful when panic creeps in. The words you repeat in your head matter more than you think. Instead of letting critical thoughts take over, "I can't do this," "Everyone's watching me mess up", replace them with phrases that bring calm and perspective. Try saying to yourself: "This is just a feeling, not a fact. I can handle this." Or, "It's okay to be nervous; it means I care." Another option: "I've gotten through tough moments before. I'll get through this, too." These phrases don't erase anxiety completely, but they take away its power to control your next move.

Sometimes, though, panic doesn't budge with quick fixes. Maybe you're in a meeting and feel heat rising up your neck, or your hands start to shake. If that happens, it's okay to step away without making a scene. You might say quietly, "I need to grab some water," or "Excuse me for a moment, I'll be right back." There's no shame in giving yourself space; most people are too caught up in their own thoughts to notice anyway. If you have a trusted colleague nearby, a work friend who gets it, a quick text or signal can bring needed backup. "Hey, can you cover for me if I need to step out?" or "Mind letting me regroup for a minute?" is sometimes all it takes.

Panic at work can feel isolating and embarrassing. Still, there's nothing wrong with needing support or asking for it when things get heavy. If these micro-habits help even once, that's progress. It's not about eliminating anxiety altogether; it's about showing yourself that with a few small moves, you can turn down the volume, even when work throws its toughest days at you.

A Practical Framework for Turning Anger Into Assertiveness

Anger isn't inherently bad; it's just a signal that something important to you is at stake. The real issue is how you handle that anger. Letting it explode in outbursts or letting it simmer into resentment only keeps you stuck. Instead, anger can fuel assertive communication, helping you express your needs without damaging relationships, like harnessing electricity: powerful when directed, dangerous when uncontrolled.

Channeling anger into assertiveness begins with recognizing it. When you notice physical signs, like a clenched jaw or a sharp tone, pause instead of reacting impulsively. Acknowledge your anger by silently stating, "I'm angry because..." For example, "I'm angry because I feel ignored in this meeting," or "I'm angry because I've picked up after everyone all week and no one's noticed." Naming your anger clarifies the emotions and prevents regrettable outbursts. Next, ask, "What do I actually need right now?" Maybe you need respect, help with chores, or to feel heard. Being clear about your need turns frustration into action.

The key move is expressing yourself assertively. Assertiveness means communicating your needs directly and respectfully, without stepping on anyone else. It's clarity without aggression, standing up for yourself while remaining honest and kind. Use straightforward scripts focused on your needs, not on blaming. For example, at work, say, "I felt frustrated when my idea was dismissed. I'd appreciate being heard out before we move on." With family, you might say, "I'm upset about how chores are divided lately. Can we talk about what's fair?" With friends: "When plans change at the last minute, I feel left out. I want to be included in decisions."

Assertive language uses "I" statements to describe specific behaviors or situations, not the other person's intentions or character. Avoid phrases like "you always" or "you never," and instead say, "When this happens, I feel..." This approach is much more likely to spark a productive conversation.

It's helpful to compare assertiveness and aggression. Imagine a colleague makes a mistake, delaying your project. An aggressive response sounds like, "You messed this up again! Why can't you ever double-check?" This approach tends to provoke defensiveness or shame.

In contrast, an assertive response is: "I noticed there was a mistake that affected our timeline. How can we prevent this next time?" This version addresses the issue without attacking, inviting collaboration.

Assertiveness also means maintaining your message even when others become defensive or dismissive. Stay calm and repeat your statement: "I want to make sure my ideas are considered," or "It's important for me that chores feel balanced." If tensions rise, suggest taking a break and resuming later.

Having scripts ready can help when emotions run high. Here are some templates you can use or modify:

- "I felt hurt when my input wasn't acknowledged. Can we talk about how we share ideas?"

- "I'm feeling overwhelmed by the extra work lately. I need some help so things feel fair."

- "When group plans change without notice, I feel left out. In the future, could we loop everyone in before deciding?"

Assertiveness keeps your boundaries intact without crossing anyone else's. It prevents grudges, focuses conversations on solutions, and avoids blame. While uncomfortable at first, especially if you're conflict-averse, it becomes easier with practice.

If you notice yourself falling back into aggressive (such as yelling or sarcasm) or passive (like silence or withdrawal) habits, remember that these are learned patterns, not unchangeable traits. Practicing assertiveness strengthens this skill over time. You'll notice better responses, faster resolutions, and leave conversations feeling respected, not resentful.

Changing your approach to anger isn't about bottling it up or pretending things are fine. It's about showing up honestly and requesting what you need with clarity, leaving drama behind. Assertiveness turns anger into a supportive ally, one honest sentence at a time.

Bounce Back by Building Everyday Emotional Resilience

Resilience isn't about acting tough or pretending you don't feel pain. It's the ability to recover after setbacks, adapt to challenges, and keep moving forward. Think of resilience as a shock absorber for your emotions. When something goes wrong at work, at home, or just in life, resilience helps you bounce back instead of getting stuck. Feeling upset, angry, or lost is normal; resilience is handling these emotions and regaining your balance over time.

Start by noticing your current reactions to setbacks. People tend to respond in different ways: some blame themselves and replay mistakes, others dive straight into problem-solving, while others seek support, and still others withdraw. Take a moment to reflect: When things go wrong, do you blame yourself, immediately try to fix things, seek help, or shut down? Recognizing your typical response is the first step towards building stronger resilience.

Use this quick self-reflection checklist:

- When plans fall apart, do I blame myself or others?

- Do I look for positives, even on tough days?

- How often do I talk things through with someone?

- Can I learn from setbacks, or do I want to move on and forget?

- Do I dwell on adverse events longer than I want to?

Building your "resilience micro-habit ladder" means adding small, supportive habits to your daily life. Start simple: at the end of each day, name one thing that went well, no matter how small. You may have completed a lingering task or shared a good laugh. These small wins shift your focus toward what's working.

Once that's comfortable, move up a rung: reframe an adverse event as a learning opportunity. Instead of "That presentation was a disaster," ask, "What could I try differently next time?" This keeps setbacks in perspective; instead of letting disappointment define you, look for what's useful and move forward.

To stretch further, try reaching out for feedback after challenging moments. Once emotions settle, ask, "Yesterday didn't go as planned, any suggestions for next time?" It's not always easy, but this habit builds confidence and shows you're open to growth.

Here are a few real-world examples. A manager faced a project failure, missed deadlines, and morale was low. Instead of blaming herself or her team, she asked everyone: What went well before things got hard? Where did we stumble? What can we try differently next time? The team felt heard, and together they improved their process and grew more connected and resilient.

Or the parent who snapped at their kids after a stressful day. Instead of dwelling in guilt, they took five minutes to breathe, identified their stress trigger, and apologized to their kids, explaining the tough day. This honest conversation didn't erase the mistake but helped everyone reset and move on.

Then there's the friend who kept struggles private but chose to open up about job stress over coffee. They weren't seeking advice; they just needed to be heard. That act of reaching out lightened their burden and offered new support for future challenging times.

Building resilience isn't about making big gestures; it's about taking small, consistent steps that count. Each rung on your habit ladder gets easier, slowly transforming how you see setbacks, not as roadblocks, but as manageable bumps along the journey.

In this chapter, we've explored how resilience helps you recover faster and face change with confidence. With tools for recognizing your habits, shifting perspective, and reaching out for support, you can steadily grow stronger. Next, we'll explore how these emotional skills contribute to creating stronger teams and fostering better collaboration at work, a setting where resilience truly makes a difference.

Chapter Four

Emotional Expression is Communicating Authentically Without Drama

The "I Feel" Formula to Express Yourself Without Blame

Have you ever stewed over a remark from someone (whether a coworker, friend, or family member) only to let your frustration erupt later, derailing the entire conversation? Maybe you've spoken up but sounded harsher than intended, or you stayed silent, letting resentment linger. Most of us weren't taught how to express complicated feelings without escalating tension. Typically, by the time we share what's bothering us, the other person gets defensive, and the talk shifts from your feelings to an argument over who's right. The "I Feel" formula is a simple tool to defuse this pattern.

The "I Feel" formula uses this structure: "I feel [emotion] when [situation] because [reason]." It's straightforward, and research supports its effectiveness. By focusing on your own feelings and experiences, rather than blaming, you reduce defensiveness and encourage open dialogue. Instead of accusations like "You never listen!" or "You always bail on plans!", which make others defensive, you communicate how something affects you, making it easier for the other person to listen without preparing to fight. Using this formula keeps conversations calm, especially when emotions run high.

Here are some examples to illustrate. At work, where meetings often run late and disrupt your schedule, you could say, "I feel frustrated when meetings go over time because I struggle to meet my deadlines." For family: "I feel hurt when you cancel dinner at the last minute because I was looking forward to catching up with you." With friends: "I feel left out when group plans change without telling me because I want to feel included." The formula strips away blame, focusing instead on your actual experience and needs.

This approach works well for everyday irritations. If your roommate never takes out the trash, instead of complaining, "You're so lazy, you never help," try, "I feel annoyed when I see the trash piling up because I want our space to feel clean and comfortable." Shifting the language creates a different energy; it's an invitation for understanding, not an attack.

It's essential to personalize the formula so it feels natural. The essence is to lead with your feelings, connect them to a specific event, and give a reason. This helps others see where you're coming from and typically invites them to share their perspective without feeling blamed.

Try It Out

Take a notebook or phone and identify three real situations, one at work, one with family, one with friends, that left you feeling upset or misunderstood. For each, write an "I Feel" statement using this formula:

- "I feel (emotion) (when) (because)."

For example:

- "I feel overlooked when my ideas aren't acknowledged in meetings because I want to contribute to our projects."

- "I feel upset when dinner plans are changed at the last minute because I plan my day around spending time together."

- "I feel anxious when texts go unanswered for days because I worry about our friendship."

Try role-playing one of these statements in a low-pressure conversation with someone you trust. Tell them you're practicing expressing yourself clearly, not starting an argument. Notice how it feels to say it; does it get easier with practice? Challenge yourself to use the formula in your next minor disagreement at home or work. Reflect on the other person's response and consider what you could improve upon.

Over time, expressing yourself this way becomes more natural. You'll notice fewer arguments and more productive conversations; people will actually listen, rather than shutting down. While it isn't a magic cure, this structure prevents emotions from becoming accusations, opening the door for honest conversations and helping both sides feel respected, even in tense moments.

Handling Emotional Overload at Home Without Yelling

That moment when everything at home feels overwhelming, the loud noise, endless chores, and scattered conversations, can push anyone to the brink. Emotional overload builds slowly until it bursts, often catching us off guard as our voices sharpen or tempers flare. Most of us don't realize we're on edge until we're already yelling or fighting tears. But if you tune into early warning signs, you can catch yourself before emotions boil over.

Your body often gives you the first clues: faster heartbeat, shallow breathing, tense jaw, clenched fists, or racing thoughts. Perhaps your voice becomes louder, or you accidentally slam things. These are red flags that you're nearing your limit. Catching them early is like spotting storm clouds before a downpour; it gives you a chance to act before things get out of control.

When you sense overload, calling a timeout can help everyone, not just you. This doesn't mean storming off or shutting down, but simply pausing before saying something you can't take back. You might say, "I need a five-minute break to calm down before we talk," or "I want to talk this through, but I'm about to lose it. Give me a few minutes, I'll come back when I'm ready." The key is not to avoid the conversation but to give yourself a chance to breathe and reset so you don't default to shouting.

Make your timeout count by actually changing your focus. Don't stew on what's upsetting you; step away from the stressor. Stepping outside for a moment of fresh air can quickly help, as can standing by an open window for a few slow breaths if going out isn't an option. Music allows some people to have a calming playlist ready for moments like these. Calming scents, like lavender, can also help ground you and cue your brain to relax. If kids are around, invite them to join you in a calming ritual: "Let's both take a deep breath and shake it out before we keep going."

Once you've calmed down, it's essential to return and re-engage. Avoiding the issue rarely works. Instead, be honest about needing space: "Thank you for giving me a minute, I was too worked up and didn't want to say something I'd regret. I'm ready to talk now." This openness shows respect and helps everyone let down their guard, making it easier to resolve things.

It can feel awkward to return to a tense conversation, especially if feelings were hurt or the topic is sensitive. Try starting with specifics: "I know we both got frustrated about the dishes earlier, can we talk now that I've cooled off?" For bigger concerns, name the tension: "That conversation hit a nerve earlier, but I want us to work through it." No need to solve everything at once; sometimes just agreeing on one small next step, like who takes out the trash or how to split chores, moves things forward.

With practice, cooling-off rituals get easier and less awkward. Stepping away before yelling and returning with honesty makes home life feel less explosive. Over time, you and your family will start to trust that you can handle challenging moments without lashing out or avoiding issues. Modeling this emotional regulation, imperfect but honest and intentional, teaches kids (and reminds adults) how to work through emotions and repair, not just react.

Spot Your Overload Signals

Take a moment to jot down your top three overload warning signs at home, body clues (like a tight chest or a quick heartbeat), habits (raising your voice, pacing), or thoughts ("If one more thing goes wrong..."). Next time you notice one, try a timeout before things escalate. Track what helps, fresh air, music, or calming scents, and what doesn't. The more you notice these patterns, the easier it becomes to avoid yelling matches and return to calm more quickly next time.

Use Apologies That Heal to Repair After Emotional Outbursts

Everyone slips up emotionally at times, snapping, shouting, or saying things they regret. Life is packed with triggers: a slammed door, a sarcastic comment that turns into an argument, or a chore dispute that escalates. If you replay these moments in your mind later and cringe, you're not alone. Outbursts don't make you a bad parent, partner, or friend; they confirm you're human. What truly matters is what happens next. Repair isn't just possible; it's what truly holds relationships together.

Many try to quickly patch things up with a rushed "Sorry" to move past the awkwardness. However, genuine apologies go deeper. A quick fix sounds like, "Sorry, can we just forget it?" but that often leaves the other person feeling dismissed. A genuine apology has three parts: you acknowledge what happened ("I yelled and that was hurtful"), recognize its impact ("You didn't deserve that; I know it upset you"), and state what you'll do differently next time. While this doesn't erase the outburst, it reopens the door to trust.

Making amends works best after everyone has cooled off. Don't push for immediate forgiveness or expect them to talk if they're still upset. Reach out with a simple message: "Can we talk about what happened earlier? I'm sorry for how I acted." Then, check in honestly with their feelings: "How did that make you feel?" and listen, really listen, without jumping in to explain or defend your actions. This is their moment to be heard.

Afterward, share your own reflection: "I realize I got loud and said things I didn't mean. That wasn't fair to you." Then outline your plan moving forward: "If I start getting upset, I'll step outside for a few minutes instead of yelling." Back your words up with effort; the follow-up matters as much as the apology. Nobody expects perfection, just sincere effort to do better.

If apologies make you feel awkward, try using simple scripts. With partners: "I'm sorry for snapping at you during our talk last night. You didn't deserve that, and I know it hurt your feelings. Next time I feel overwhelmed, I'll ask for a break instead." With kids or teens, who are often sensitive to tone, try: "I shouldn't have raised my voice like that earlier. It probably felt harsh, and I'm working on handling things better when I'm stressed." For roommates after a shouting match about chores: "I overreacted about the kitchen mess. That wasn't fair. Let's set a time each week to clean together so it doesn't build up."

Work settings require humility and clarity. If you lose your temper under deadline pressure, try: "I apologize for losing my temper in the meeting. My words were sharp and probably made things worse. Next time, I'll step back to cool off before we continue." For friends, if you've been impatient or sarcastic: "Hey, I was short with you over text yesterday. Sorry, I was frustrated about something else and took it out on you."

Sometimes, especially after bigger blowups, the other person needs time before they're ready to talk or forgive. Respect their space, but check back in; don't just leave things unresolved. Say, "I want us to be good again whenever you're ready." If they later bring up your outburst, don't respond with "That was ages ago!" Acknowledge their lingering feelings.

Repair isn't about erasing mistakes; it's about rebuilding trust gradually after each misstep. Over time, consistent acts of repair help create a safe climate where everyone is less afraid of permanent relationship damage from outbursts. The more often you practice honest apologies and follow through, the easier it is for you and those around you.

Apologies are more than just words; they're a way to show people they matter enough for you to try again. And if you slip up once more? Start over, acknowledge it, own it, and keep trying. That's what real emotional growth looks like in everyday life.

Finding Your Voice at Work: Be Assertive, Not Aggressive

Standing up for yourself at work can feel risky, especially if you're unsure where the line between assertive and aggressive behavior actually lies. Perhaps you've witnessed someone in a meeting interrupt others or heard a coworker snap, "You always dump things on me!" That's aggression, pushing your frustration onto others, which usually puts them on the defensive or even shuts them down. Assertiveness, though, is entirely different. It's about stating your needs and opinions clearly, without stomping on anyone else's toes. You might say, "I'd like to discuss my workload," instead of accusing your boss, "You're giving me way too much work." One asks for a conversation, the other blames. Aggression can create conflict and resentment, while assertiveness opens the door to honest discussion and solutions. This difference matters even more for women, who often get labeled as "difficult" or "bossy" for speaking up. At the same time, aggressive men sometimes get away with it. No one wants to be the office bulldozer, but you also don't want to fade into the background when your needs matter.

Preparing to be assertive starts before you say a word. Get clear on what you actually want, whether it's a deadline extension, a fair workload, recognition on a project, or just to be heard in meetings. If you're unsure, jot down your thoughts before the conversation. What's the real need? Sometimes it's not only about the workload; it could be about feeling respected or wanting clarity. Once you know your goal, plan how you'll say it. Direct language works best: be specific without apologizing or tiptoeing around your message. Replace phrases like "Sorry, but..." or "I don't mean to bother you" with "I need" or "I'd like." Your voice should sound steady and calm, not rushed, not harsh.

Let's look at a few real-life scripts you can use on the job. If you need more time on a project, instead of waiting until the last minute or panicking in silence, say to your manager: "I've reviewed the project requirements and need an extra two days to deliver my best work. Is that possible?" This approach is clear about your needs and shows responsibility. When a colleague keeps interrupting in meetings, try: "I'd like to finish my thought before we move on." It's concise and direct, eliminating the need for apologies or sarcasm. If a peer isn't pulling their weight on a group project, say: "I noticed some tasks are still outstanding. Can we review responsibilities so we're all clear moving forward?" This keeps the tone professional while addressing the real issue.

Sometimes you'll have to ask for something that feels even more loaded, like a raise or promotion. Here's a script for that: "I'd like to talk about my growth here and review my compensation. Over the past year, I've taken on additional projects and consistently met targets." Notice there's no apology or tentativeness. You state facts and open up the topic for discussion.

Of course, not everyone will respond well to assertiveness at first. You might get interrupted, brushed off, or even told to "relax." In those moments, don't shrink away. Reiterate your point: "I'd like to finish what I was saying," or "This is important to me, can we discuss it now or schedule a time?" If someone dismisses your request for help with deadlines or workload, say, "I understand if now isn't possible, but I need to know when we can talk about this." Keep your voice steady; don't let eye rolls or sighs distract you.

To get comfortable with this style of communication, rehearse statements out loud before meetings or difficult conversations. You can role-play with a friend or practice in front of a mirror. Imagine pushback and plan your response. Will you repeat your request, ask clarifying questions, or suggest another time to talk? Write down three statements you want to try this week: one for making a request, one for addressing an issue with a colleague, and one for giving feedback. Jot down what went well after each conversation and what you'd tweak next time.

If your assertiveness is repeatedly ignored or dismissed, don't blame yourself. Sometimes work cultures reward silence or conflict avoidance. If that's the case, look for allies, others who share your concerns, and brainstorm how to raise issues together or escalate them respectfully if needed.

Assertiveness is a skill that grows with each attempt. With practice, you'll notice more respect from others and more confidence in yourself. Over time, speaking up will feel less risky and more like second nature, even when nerves creep in.

Navigating Emotional Conversations With Kids and Teens

Talking about feelings with kids and teens can feel like walking through a maze blindfolded. Many adults freeze, worry about saying the wrong thing, or don't know where to start. You might worry about making things worse, or you might remember how awkward it felt when your own parents tried to talk about emotions. Often, we slip into lecture mode or try to fix everything, only to be met with silence, eye rolls, or doors slamming. The truth is, most of us didn't grow up having open talks about feelings, so it's no surprise we struggle to create those conversations now. Yet, whether you're a parent, stepparent, aunt, uncle, or caregiver, these moments are worth the effort. Kids and teens who feel safe expressing emotions build stronger coping skills and deeper connections, both with themselves and with you.

One of the biggest challenges is knowing how to translate your feelings into language your child will actually understand. With younger children, please keep it simple and concrete. Short sentences work best, and naming your own feelings helps them learn how to name theirs. For example, if your child is melting down after a tough day at school, you might say, "I can see you're upset. Sometimes I feel sad too when things don't go my way." If your child shouts or acts out, try: "I feel sad when you shout because I want us to talk calmly." It's not about scolding, it's about showing them there's a name for what's happening inside.

With tweens and teens, the language shifts. They're more sensitive to tone and quick to spot insincerity or judgment. Avoid lectures or loaded questions like "What's wrong with you?" Instead, be specific and honest without sounding accusatory. For instance: "I'm worried when you don't come home on time because I care about your safety." Or if your teen seems distant: "I notice you've been quiet lately. I'm here if you want to talk." Teens often test boundaries and may push back on emotional conversations. That's normal; they're learning how to handle big feelings just like adults.

Making these talks less intimidating can help everyone relax. Try turning emotional sharing into a game or daily ritual. For younger kids, "feelings charades" works wonders, take turns acting out emotions (happy, angry, scared) and guessing what they are. This gets everyone laughing and builds emotional vocabulary without pressure. For older kids and teens, consider "emotion check-in" cards. Write down different feeling words on slips of paper (e.g., worried, excited, annoyed, proud), toss them into a bowl, and take turns picking one to describe a recent situation where that feeling arose. You might be surprised at what surfaces in these low-key moments.

Resistance is going to happen; kids might clam up, roll their eyes, or act like they don't care. When a child withdraws or storms off, avoid chasing them down or demanding answers right away. Instead, leave the door open: "I'm here when you're ready to talk," or "If you want to chat later, just let me know." This gives them space while letting them know you care. If your teen vents and then retreats behind headphones, respect their need for distance but come back later: "Earlier seemed tough, I'm still here if you want to talk." Modeling calm after a blowup is powerful; when your teen sees you regrouping without holding a grudge, it teaches them that emotional storms can pass and relationships can recover.

Interactive exercises can break the cycle of tension and silence. Some families create a "feelings wall" where everyone adds sticky notes with emotions or thoughts from the week, no discussion required unless someone wants it. Others use car rides for check-ins; talking while looking out the window makes things less intense for many kids. Even texting can work for teens who are more comfortable typing than talking face-to-face.

If your child's resistance lasts longer than usual or shuts down every connection attempt, don't take it personally. Some kids process emotions slowly or need time before they're ready to share. Continue showing up with small gestures, such as leaving a snack on their desk, sharing a funny meme, or simply sitting nearby, so they know you're not giving up on them.

What matters most in these conversations isn't getting every word perfect but showing up with honesty and patience. Your willingness to discuss feelings, even if it's awkward, lays the foundation for stronger communication as your child grows older.

As we wrap up this chapter on emotional expression, take a breath and remind yourself that none of these skills require perfection, just effort and openness. Whether at home, work, or in friendships, sharing emotions authentically is key to building trust and connection. Next, we'll explore how empathy transforms conversations and helps us bridge gaps with others, even when words fall short.

Chapter Five

Empathy in Action to Bridge the Empathy Gap

Spotting Nonverbal Emotional Cues by Reading Between the Lines

Imagine catching up with a friend at your favorite café. She says she's "fine," but her eyes flick away, her shoulders slump, and her mouth forms a thin line. You wonder if you should ask if she's okay, but you're unsure; maybe you're misreading her. The reality is, we all pick up on nonverbal cues constantly, sometimes unconsciously. These signals, stance, voice changes, and an eyebrow twitch form the emotional subtext of every conversation, often saying more than words ever could. It's a universal language we all speak, connecting us in our shared human experience.

Learning to read body language begins with tuning in to the basics. Facial expressions are especially telling. Furrowed brows indicate possible confusion, anger, or concentration, while raised eyebrows may show surprise or skepticism. Tight lips or a clenched jaw often reveal frustration or discomfort. Posture also speaks volumes: crossed arms usually mean defensiveness or withdrawal; slouched shoulders suggest sadness or defeat. Fidgeting (tapping, bouncing legs, playing with jewelry) tends to signal anxiety or impatience. Small gestures can reveal much about a person's true feelings.

Tone of voice is equally important. A flat, monotone delivery might hint at boredom or sadness, while a clipped tone often means irritation or stress. People may talk faster when nervous, or speak in whispers or cracking voices when vulnerable or scared. Laughter can also be telling, genuine and relaxed, or anxious and forced. Often, *how* something is said matters more than *what* is said.

To refine your skills, try doing a "nonverbal scan" during conversations. First, notice eye contact: are they looking at you or avoiding your gaze (which could mean discomfort or distraction)? Intense staring might suggest confrontation or deep focus. Observe posture: leaning in means engagement, leaning away suggests disinterest. An open stance means receptiveness; a closed posture (arms crossed, feet turned away) may indicate resistance or discomfort. Listen for tone changes: shifts in softness, sharpness, or speed can signal emotional changes. Lastly, note physical distance: sitting closer generally signals comfort; moving away may mean discomfort or a desire for privacy.

You don't need to be Sherlock Holmes to practice this skill. Try watching TV with the sound off and guessing characters' emotions from their faces and gestures. Observe colleagues' body language: who leans forward in meetings, who seems checked out? At home, watch your kids at dinner or bedtime: do they fidget when nervous, avoid eye contact when hiding something, or flop onto the couch when exhausted? Practicing in low-pressure situations makes recognizing these cues in honest conversations much easier.

But beware of pitfalls: not everyone's body language matches textbook norms. Culture significantly affects what cues mean; averted eyes can mean nervousness in one culture and respectful listening in another.

Neurodiversity matters, too: some people naturally avoid eye contact or fidget, no matter their mood. Personality plays a role; introverts may appear withdrawn when simply deep in thought. If you're unsure, check assumptions gently by saying things like, "You got quiet, something on your mind?" or "You seem tense; am I reading that right?" This encourages openness and helps avoid misunderstandings.

Nonverbal Cues Observation Challenge

For the next three days, try spotting three nonverbal cues each day, at home, work, or in public. Make a note: Were their arms crossed? Change in tone? A smile that didn't reach the eyes? Write one sentence about what you think it meant, and how you responded or wanted to respond. At day's end, reflect: Did your guesses match what people said they felt? Were you sometimes wrong? The aim isn't perfection but curiosity and improved empathy.

Genuine empathy goes beyond just listening; it's about noticing what's unsaid and showing you care enough to ask. Even if you misread cues, paying attention lets people feel seen and understood. It's this kind of empathetic communication that can genuinely transform relationships and make the world a more compassionate place. So, let's strive to be better listeners, to read between the lines, and to show we care.

How to Listen Without Fixing Using "Holding Space"

Have you ever tried to open up about something challenging, only to have the other person jump in with a solution or a story about themselves? You end up feeling brushed aside, not really heard. This is where "holding space" comes in; it's the simple but powerful act of being fully present for someone without rushing in to fix, judge, or hijack the conversation. When you hold space, you give that person room to feel, reflect, and process, knowing they're not alone. It's a powerful tool of empathy, one that can transform relationships and bring comfort in times of need.

The '3 C's' can make holding space less mysterious and much more doable. **Curiosity** is first. Instead of mentally scripting your response or solution, focus on asking gentle, open questions. These aren't meant to dig for details or satisfy your own curiosity, but to help the other person explore what's inside them. You might say, 'How did that feel for you?' or 'What was the hardest part?' This shows you care about their experience and are willing to listen without an agenda. Next is **Compassion**. This is the core of holding space, showing genuine care without rushing to judge or minimize their feelings. Compassion sounds like, 'That sounds really hard,' or, 'I'm so sorry you're going through this.' You don't need a fix; your honest empathy is enough. Lastly, **Containment** is the trickiest part. It's resisting the urge to jump in with reassurance, advice, or your own stories. You might feel uncomfortable with silence or pain, but reminding yourself that it's not your job to rescue or direct the conversation helps you stay grounded and supportive.

When you're listening to someone who's sharing something painful or vulnerable, it can be tempting to fill the silence or shift the focus. But often, the most meaningful support comes from simple phrases that acknowledge what they're experiencing without changing the subject or handing out solutions. Try these on for size: "That sounds really tough," "I'm here if you want to talk more," or "It makes sense you'd feel that way." If you're not sure what to say, just naming what you notice, "I can see this is weighing on you", can go a long way. If they pause or cry, just being present with a gentle nod or steady eye contact lets them know you aren't going anywhere.

It helps to keep a mental checklist of do's and don'ts when holding space. Do stay focused on them, nod occasionally, keep your posture open, and reflect back what you hear: "It sounds like you felt really let down." Silence is not awkward if it gives them space to think or feel. Don't jump in with advice unless they specifically ask for it; most people want empathy first and solutions later. Avoid changing the subject or telling a story about your own similar experience; this can feel like you're steering attention away from them. Comparing struggles ("That happened to me too!") usually falls flat and can even make someone feel small for sharing.

The Holding Space Checklist

Don't nod and use an open posture. Interrupt with advice. Reflect back feelings ("I hear you felt..."). Shift focus to yourself. Stay quiet and let them lead. Change the subject abruptly. Ask open-ended questions ("What helped?"). Compare struggles ("Me too!"). Allow silence. Minimize their feelings ("It's not so bad")

Holding space doesn't mean agreeing with everything or pretending to have all the answers. It's about giving people the dignity of their own process and letting them know their feelings matter. Even if all you say is, "Thanks for telling me," you're showing up in a way that builds trust and genuine connection. The next time someone shares something difficult with you, try setting aside your inner fixer and just be there, fully present. Often, that's precisely what they need most.

Scripts for Family and Work Using Empathy in Tough Talks

When stakes are high and emotions run strong, empathy is what turns tough conversations into moments of understanding instead of conflict. Think back to a time you needed to address something uncomfortable with your partner, maybe after a heated argument, when they went quiet and pulled away. Or imagine having to face a coworker to discuss a mistake that impacted the entire project. These situations make your heart race and mind spin, you worry about hurt feelings, misunderstanding, or making things worse. It's common to freeze or avoid the talk, wishing issues would resolve themselves, but avoidance rarely works. What actually helps is beginning the conversation with empathy, showing right away you care about their feelings and want to understand their side, even when you need to set boundaries or disagree.

Here's a simple formula for starting tough talks with empathy:

- **Name what you observe** – "I can tell this is weighing on you" or

"I noticed you seemed upset after the meeting."

- **Validate their feelings** – "That must be tough" or "I imagine this isn't easy."

- **Express your intention to listen** – "I want to hear your perspective."

This slows things down, lowers defenses, and opens honest, blame-free space. You're not trying to fix everything at once, just letting them know their feelings are valid.

Let's look at real scripts you can use. At home, if your partner has been distant after a disagreement, try: "I notice you've been quiet since our talk earlier. I care about how you're feeling and want to understand what's going on for you." This isn't an accusation, it's a gentle invitation to share, showing you're there to listen, not just defend your view. If your partner gives short answers or avoids talking, refrain from pushing. Instead, say, "It's okay if you don't want to talk right now. I'm here whenever you're ready." Sometimes just offering patience helps someone open up.

At work, conversations are often even more challenging with pride and reputation at stake. Suppose a teammate misses a deadline and seems defeated. In that case, you might say, "I know the feedback we got stung, and I'm sure this is stressful. How are you holding up?" or "I noticed you seemed frustrated after that email. Do you want to talk about it?" You're not excusing mistakes, but you focus on their experience first. This helps them let down their guard and work on solutions, instead of getting stuck in shame or blame.

Sometimes, empathy won't instantly solve things. People may still become defensive, angry, or withdraw, especially if they feel embarrassed. If so, don't push or justify yourself repeatedly. Respect their limits: "I can see this is a lot right now. If you need space, I get it. Let me know when you're ready to continue." Letting someone decide when to talk can be a huge relief and builds trust.

Empathy also matters when setting boundaries, not just when someone is hurting. Say you need to ask your sibling to stop late-night calls. Try, "I know you've had a lot going on lately, and I want to support you. I'm finding the late calls hard during the workweek. Can we find another time that works for us?" You're acknowledging their need and also honoring your own; this is empathy as action.

If someone resists by deflecting, changing the subject, or lashing out, resist being drawn into an argument. Pause and say, "It seems like this isn't a good time to talk. I respect that." If they later come back (as often happens), respond warmly: "Thanks for coming back to this, I appreciate it." That small patience matters.

Perfection isn't required for empathy to have an impact. Even awkward efforts can help soften tense moments. Practicing these scripts, in family life or under work pressure, makes them easier when the real tests come. If your goal is connection, not just being right, you're already ahead in challenging conversations.

Avoiding the Empathy Trap With Boundaries for the Emotionally Sensitive

If you're someone who feels everything deeply, you may know the "empathy trap," even if you haven't called it that. It happens when your desire to help others leaves you feeling exhausted, resentful, or guilty for needing a break. Maybe you spend hours comforting a friend after their breakup and wake up irritable, or your coworker's daily venting leaves you unable to focus or enjoy your downtime. What starts as compassion becomes a burden, carrying the emotions of others alongside your own. Over time, unlimited caring can deplete you. This is the empathy trap: a cycle where kindness turns to exhaustion or resentment.

Start by recognizing the signs of empathy burnout. It often creeps up quietly. You might feel irritable after long calls, dread reading texts because they bring more problems, or notice a lingering heaviness even after helping someone. You may dread talking to certain people, or feel trapped by guilt for wanting to say "no." Burnout isn't just tiredness, but emotional depletion. Physical symptoms, such as headaches, insomnia, or shoulder tension, may appear. If you're always listening but never feel heard, or if you feel resentful or snap at loved ones, burnout could be at play.

To assess your boundaries, ask yourself: Do I feel lighter or heavier after helping? Am I saying yes when I want to say no? Do certain people leave me drained? Is my self-care slipping? If you answer yes to several of these questions, you may be giving away too much emotional energy and need to step back.

Setting limits can feel selfish, especially if you're used to putting others first. But boundaries keep your empathy healthy and sustainable. Remember: you can't pour from an empty cup. Saying no, or stepping back, is okay. Try gentle scripts like, "I care about you, but I need to take care of myself right now," or "I want to help, but can't give this my full attention today." For coworkers: "I can listen for a few minutes, but then I need to get back to work." For family: "I know this is tough. Can we talk later, when I have more energy?" These responses acknowledge others' feelings while respecting your own limits.

Use body language and routines to reinforce boundaries. For example, at work, if someone wants to vent at your desk, stand up or let them know you're headed somewhere. At home, step outside or put on headphones when you need space; non-verbal cues show you're taking a break from emotional labor. If guilt arises, remind yourself that boundaries aren't rejection, but a form of self-respect.

After emotionally charged interactions, take steps to refill your own tank. Self-care doesn't have to be elaborate; sometimes, a five-minute walk after a tough call is enough to reset your mood. Journaling helps too; jot down your feelings or what you wish you'd said. Even a few sentences can help process your emotions and prevent them from lingering. Scheduling quiet time before or after social events, reading for ten minutes before heading home, or sitting in silence with tea after dinner can buffer your energy.

Experiment with different recovery routines to see what helps most. Some people need movement, others crave stillness. Try music, meditation, watering plants, or watching a favorite show. The goal is not to erase fatigue entirely, but to respect and replenish yourself, so you can offer empathy from a place of actual presence and care, not just out of obligation.

Closing the Empathy Gap in Digital Communication

Empathy can feel almost slippery online. So much of what helps us connect in person, subtle facial shifts, body language, a gentle tone, is missing when we send a text or dash off an email. You've probably had moments where you read a message and wondered, "Are they mad at me?" Or you've sent a quick reply, only to realize later it came across as cold or dismissive. Group chats and email threads are notorious for sparking confusion. Sometimes, silence in a team chat makes you worry someone's upset, when really, they're just swamped or distracted. Without the cues our brains rely on, we're left filling in the blanks, often with worst-case scenarios. Misunderstandings grow faster in these digital spaces, especially if you're already tired or stressed.

To bridge this empathy gap, you need to bring extra care and clarity to your virtual words. One easy way is to pay attention to your tone and add warmth where it's needed. Emojis, used mindfully, can go a long way in showing positive intent ("Thanks for your help " feels friendlier than just "Thanks."). You can also be explicit about your mood or meaning: "I'm excited to be part of this!" or "No pressure, just checking in." These small touches help others read you more accurately. When someone seems quiet online, don't assume the worst. A gentle check-in like, "Hey, I noticed you've been quiet lately, just wanted to see how you're doing," lets people know you care without putting them on the spot. Sometimes people need space, but your outreach still matters.

When tension creeps in, perhaps there has been a sharp exchange or a message left hanging. Addressing it directly but gently helps restore trust. If you think you have misunderstood someone, try saying, "I may have misread your message. Can we clear things up?" This opens the door for honest conversation without blame. If group chat silence leaves everyone uneasy, a simple, "I noticed things got quiet after my last message, just checking in to see if everything's okay," signals you're open to feedback and care about the group's mood. For emotionally charged emails, take a moment to acknowledge the emotion behind the words: "I can see this topic is frustrating, I'm here to help sort it out." These templates soften edges and turn misunderstandings into honest conversations.

Another valuable digital empathy skill is learning to pause before responding, what I like to call a "digital pause." When you receive a message that stings or confuses you, don't rush to reply. Instead, stop and breathe. Please read the message once, set your phone down or look away for a moment, then reread it with fresh eyes. Ask yourself: "How might they be feeling? Is there another way to interpret this?" Only then should you write your response. This small buffer gives your brain time to cool off and reflect, so you're less likely to react defensively or escalate things by accident. If emotions are running high, draft your reply and come back to it after a short break.

Digital communication throws curveballs, a joke might miss, feedback can sound harsh, or a request gets lost in translation. Practicing empathy online means being willing to clarify your intentions and check in with others instead of making assumptions. It's about using words as clearly as possible while remembering there's a real person on the other side of the screen.

Remember that whether face-to-face or online, understanding others takes effort but pays off in trust and connection. Bringing empathy into digital spaces doesn't have to be complicated; you need awareness, patience, and the willingness to reach out when something feels off. Next up, we'll dig into how these empathy skills can fuel better teamwork and stronger collaboration at work and at home, so you can not only connect but also achieve more together.

Chapter Six

Communication That Connects With Active Listening, Feedback, and Conflict

The "Active Listening" Blueprint for Work and Relationships

Have you ever nodded along during a conversation, only to realize your thoughts were elsewhere, or offered a distracted "uh-huh" while someone vented? Maybe in meetings you half-listen, just catching the main points while missing colleagues' real feelings and concerns. There's a big difference between simply hearing words and truly listening. Hearing is passive; you notice sounds without full attention. Active listening, on the other hand, is intentional; it's about tuning in not just to words but to moods and meanings, making the other person feel valued and understood. In our distraction-filled lives, genuine, focused listening is rare, and feels meaningful when someone offers it.

Active listening means being present, rather than simply waiting to respond or solve a problem. At home, it helps your partner feel that you genuinely care. At work, it builds trust among colleagues and makes meetings more productive. In friendships, it turns small talk into lasting bonds. What matters is making others feel seen and respected. Communication experts agree: being fully present and reflecting back understanding deepens trust and reduces misunderstandings. By actively listening, you can avoid misinterpretations and ensure that your message is received as intended.

How do you break old habits and actually practice active listening? Start by removing distractions, put away your phone, shut your laptop, and turn off notifications if you're engaging with someone at work or home. Make comfortable eye contact to show you're paying attention. Next, paraphrase what the speaker said: for example, "So the new project deadline feels impossible given your current workload?" This helps you stay engaged while letting the other person clarify any misunderstandings.

Then, reflect the speaker's feelings. This doesn't mean acting as a therapist; it's enough to notice, "You sound frustrated," or "I can tell this is stressing you out." Often, people want their emotions acknowledged rather than fixed. Afterward, check for accuracy by asking, "Did I get that right?" or "Is that how you're feeling?" This feedback loop keeps the conversation honest and shows you value what they're saying.

To build these skills, practice them with someone close to you, about a minor annoyance or an everyday issue. As they talk, please go through the steps: minimize distractions, paraphrase their story, reflect their feelings, and check your understanding. Or, in a meeting with a coworker, try active listening when discussing a challenge: "I hear you're worried about finishing on time," then follow up with, "Is something specific getting in the way?" Practicing on simple topics builds confidence for more challenging conversations.

Real life isn't always tidy; sometimes your mind wanders, especially if you're tired or distracted. When this happens, use a quick reset (take a breath or touch something on your desk) to refocus. If you lose track or feel confused, ask for clarification: "Could you say more about that?" or "I want to make sure I'm following, can you give me an example?" These prompts keep you engaged and demonstrate that you care about truly understanding.

Impatience can block good listening, especially if you want to offer advice or hurry the process. Remind yourself that silence is valuable; people often need a moment to gather their thoughts. Instead of filling every pause, allow space for the other person to continue or explain further.

Active Listening

The Active Listening is a great way to put your skills to the test. Pick one daily conversation, at work or home, where you'll use all four steps of active listening:

- eliminate distractions.

- paraphrase.

- reflect feelings.

- check for understanding.

Afterwards, jot down how the exchange felt for both you and the other person. Notice if the conversation went more smoothly or if the other person seemed more open. This challenge not only helps you practice active listening but also allows you to see the immediate benefits in your relationships and interactions.

Practicing these steps may feel awkward at first, but that's normal. Over time, they'll become natural, and others will notice. Even in routine moments, such as family dinners or conversations with friends, these skills help make conversations more meaningful and reduce misunderstandings. Whether at home or at work, active listening builds trust and fosters connections that endure long after a single conversation.

How to Give and Receive Without Drama With Feedback That Lands

Giving feedback can be challenging. If it's too vague, it's useless; too blunt, and it may cause defensiveness. Criticism like "You're always late" or "You never listen" rarely leads to real change, just resistance. Effective feedback is specific, focused on behaviors, actionable, and leads to a clear next step. Rather than hinting or circling around issues, give direct information people can use to improve. The **SBIR** approach, **S**ituation, **B**ehavior, **I**mpact, **R**equest, makes feedback more productive both at work and at home.

Please describe the situation to clarify where and when the behavior happened, then address the behavior itself (what the person did, not their character). Next, explain the impact of their actions, and finally, make your request for future behavior. This structure clears up misunderstandings and helps everyone stay focused. For example: "During our Monday meeting (Situation), you interrupted several times while others spoke (Behavior). That made it hard for everyone to share their ideas (Impact). Could you wait until each person finishes before responding next time? (Request)." At home, you might say, "Last night at dinner (Situation), you were on your phone while we talked (Behavior). It felt like you weren't really present (Impact). Can we agree to keep phones away during meals? (Request)."

These templates simplify tough conversations and help you organize thoughts, avoiding emotional diversions. Try basic scripts like: "When you [behavior], I noticed [impact]. Could we try [request]?" In a family: "When you leave dishes in the sink overnight, I feel overwhelmed in the morning. Can you rinse them before bed?" At work: "When you send last-minute updates, I have to scramble to adjust. Could you send them earlier in the day?"

Receiving feedback, especially critical feedback, can be just as tough. It's easy to react defensively or to dismiss what's being said. Instead, listen fully, even if it's uncomfortable. Summarize what you heard ("So you're saying my emails seem rushed?"). This checks for understanding and shows you're engaged. If you're unclear, ask for examples: "Can you give a specific time that happened?" This grounds feedback in concrete reality.

Thanking someone for their feedback ("Thanks for letting me know" or "I appreciate your honesty") keeps the exchange open, even if it stings. You don't have to agree immediately. It's fine to pause and reflect: "I hear what you're saying and want to think about how I can use this." Decide later which points actually help you.

Not all feedback is delivered well; sometimes people lash out or speak up when they're upset. If it feels unfair, avoid reacting immediately. You can say, "I'm feeling defensive now. Can we talk later?" Allowing time can transform a heated moment into a productive exchange. Asking to follow up signals respect and keeps conversations constructive.

Feedback may sting, no matter how it's delivered; that's a sign you care about your work or relationships. Still, not every comment needs to be taken to heart. After the initial reaction passes, sort out what's helpful versus what's not. Sometimes, criticism reflects the other person's stress or perspective, rather than the absolute truth.

Giving feedback in the heat of the moment, when everyone's tired or emotional, rarely ends well. Wait until things have cooled off: "Let's talk about this tomorrow when we're both less tired." Bringing up issues later, with specifics and a cooperative attitude, makes it more likely you'll be truly heard.

Treat feedback as a tool for building relationships, not just calling out flaws. Used well, it helps everyone do better, at home, at work, anywhere people want to improve. Awkward conversations get easier when you're clear, respectful, and both sides know what to expect.

De-Escalation Scripts for Heated Family Arguments

Arguments at home rarely begin as shouting matches. They build, moment by moment, from little frictions, maybe a loaded sigh, a sarcastic jab, or an eye roll. Before you know it, the energy in the room shifts. You might catch yourself clenching your fists, pacing, or stewing in silence. Voices rise, each person fighting to be heard, and interruptions start stacking up. These are the warning signals that an argument is about to get out of control: sarcasm slipping in, the pace of speaking getting faster, or someone storming out mid-sentence. If you notice your heart pounding, breathing faster, or your hands shaking, these physical cues are your body's alarm bells. Even just feeling your jaw tighten or noticing that you're repeating yourself means escalation is happening. Recognizing these signs can save you from saying things you'll regret later.

When you spot arguments heating up, having ready language and a clear plan can make all the difference. Instead of pushing through full speed ahead, call a brief "time-out." You can say, "I want us to work through this, but I need a few minutes to calm down." It feels awkward at first, maybe even like you're avoiding the problem, but it actually keeps things from spiraling. Sometimes just naming what's happening, "We're both getting upset right now; let's pause before this gets worse", lowers the temperature instantly. If you're able, suggest a short break: "Let's each take ten minutes and come back." Move to another room or go outside for a breath of fresh air. This isn't about running away; it's about giving your brain and body space to reset.

Not every argument stops just because one person calls for a break. Accusations and blame can keep flying. When you're on the receiving end of harsh words or finger-pointing, it's easy to get swept up and fire back. Instead, try grounding yourself with a steady breath and respond with empathy, even if you're not feeling it in the moment. Say something like, "I can see this is really important to you. Let's both take a breath." That single sentence can short-circuit an emotional explosion. Or use, "I hear you. Can we focus on one thing at a time?" This gently redirects the conversation without dismissing their feelings. These phrases help keep you steady and prevent things from escalating into a bigger fight.

If you find yourself spiraling, raising your voice, using sarcasm, or feeling like leaving, pause and check in with yourself. Sometimes just having a physical cue helps: touch your thumb to your finger, take three deep breaths, or even splash water on your face. The trick isn't to stop feeling angry or hurt but to interrupt the automatic cycle that leads to saying things you regret. You might also find it helpful to say out loud, "I want to fix this, but I need a second to cool off." This shows you care about the relationship more than being right in the moment.

Once everyone has taken time apart and emotions aren't running so high, how you return matters just as much as how you paused. Don't skip straight back into the argument like nothing happened. Instead, set up a small family "reset", maybe gather in the living room or around the kitchen table. Start with something positive before diving back in, such as sharing one thing you appreciate about each other or recalling a recent team or family win. It could sound like, "Before we talk about what happened earlier, I want to say I really value how hard we're all trying." This changes the emotional tone and reminds everyone that connection comes first.

You could make it a mini-ritual: after every heated argument, agree to schedule a follow-up chat that begins with each person saying one good thing about the other or themselves, no matter how basic. Then revisit the challenging topic with calmer minds. Try saying, "I know we were both upset before; I'd like to hear your side now that we've both had time." Or use, "What matters most to you about this issue?" This opens space for honesty without judgment.

Family conflicts are messy by nature; nobody gets it perfect every time. But learning these scripts and routines gives you tools to change old patterns, moving arguments from shouting and blame toward understanding and repair. It's not about suppressing strong feelings; it's about making space for them without letting them destroy trust or closeness. Over time, these small changes shift the atmosphere at home and help everyone feel heard, even in the middle of disagreement.

Navigating Group Dynamics to Handle Tension in Teams

In team meetings, much of the real conversation happens beneath the surface, through side chats, exchanged glances, or subtle gestures like eye rolls and muttered comments. Group communication hinges as much on what remains unspoken as on what is openly shared. Unchecked power struggles, hidden agendas, or groupthink can quickly entangle even well-meaning teams, leading to misunderstandings and missed opportunities.

Tension in groups is rarely blatant. Instead, it emerges through subtle behaviors, such as someone dominating the discussion, managers pushing decisions without seeking input, or a few voices fading into the background. When controversial topics arise, members may avoid disagreement, creating a false sense of consensus. Signs such as crossed arms, averted eyes, or rapid topic changes can go unnoticed until they snowball into major issues.

An effective way to surface concerns early is to start meetings with a round-robin check-in, giving everyone a brief chance to share their thoughts about the work at hand. Even a simple "red/yellow/green" system, red for major worries, yellow for caution, green for all clear, can air issues before they stew into resentment. Another tip: set explicit group norms at the outset regarding how the team will address disagreement, interruptions, and decision-making. Establishing these expectations creates a foundation for accountability in the event of challenges.

If tension bubbles up during a meeting, perhaps after someone shares a bold idea and the group falls silent, don't brush it aside. Instead, address it directly and respectfully. For example, say, "I sense there's some disagreement. Can we talk about what's not being said?" This approach allows for honest feedback without making anyone feel targeted. If you notice side conversations or disengagement, pause and say, "Let's make sure everyone feels heard before we move forward." These subtle resets can shift group dynamics and give quieter members room to speak.

Managing difficult personalities is part of the process. Some people naturally dominate, while others rarely contribute unless prompted. If you're leading, directly ask, "I'd like to hear from some folks we haven't heard yet," or, when not in charge, suggest, "I'm curious if anyone who hasn't spoken has thoughts on this." These prompts show that all perspectives are valued.

Adding structure can help balance participation. A talking stick, physical or digital, limits conversation to one person at a time, reducing interruptions and making it safer for everyone to contribute. Assigning a facilitator for each meeting ensures that someone is actively monitoring for dominating or silencing behaviors and maintaining a fair discussion. If discussions heat up or get stuck, a neutral party can steer the group back on track: "Let's return to the agenda and ensure all viewpoints are included."

When obvious power dynamics discourage open disagreement, such as when someone's title intimidates others, address it directly: "I know I have strong opinions, but I want to hear different perspectives." While this won't guarantee immediate honesty, it encourages more open and authentic debate.

Hidden agendas can undermine progress; team members may stay quiet out of fear of looking bad or losing influence. If there's resistance beneath the surface, invite transparency: "If anyone has hesitations or concerns about our direction, now's the time to share." By framing disagreement as valuable, not disruptive, you help make honest input safer.

Team Dynamics Reflection

After your next meeting, jot down three observations: Who talked most? Who stayed quiet? Did you notice tension (body language, sighs, quick topic changes)? Identify one thing you could do next time to help balance participation or surface hidden concerns.

All teams face challenges, but with slight shifts in awareness and communication, tension can become a driver for progress rather than a source of dysfunction. By paying attention to both spoken and unspoken dynamics and inviting input from all members, teams can become more honest and effective.

What to Say After Something Goes Wrong, or, How to Repair and Reconnect

In every relationship, mistakes happen, harsh words, missed cues, or misplaced stress are part of life, no matter your emotional intelligence. The important part isn't perfection, but knowing how to rebuild trust and connection after things go wrong. Mistakes don't mean the relationship is broken; repairs are opportunities to deepen trust. Addressing problems, rather than ignoring them, shows you care about the relationship.

Repairing isn't some mystical process; it's a skill anyone can learn, regardless of how awkward apologies might feel. It involves three straightforward steps: acknowledge, apologize, and ask or act.

First, acknowledge what happened by naming the issue directly, without excuses or sugarcoating. For example: "I realize I hurt you when I canceled at the last minute," or "I snapped at you in front of the team." Simply naming the problem shows maturity and respect.

Second, offer a genuine apology. Avoid phrases like "I'm sorry you felt that way," which can come across as dismissive. Instead, keep it sincere and direct: "I'm sorry. That wasn't fair to you," or "I regret how I handled that." Match your words to your tone; people know when you're just trying to move on or avoid discomfort.

The final step is repair through concrete action. Ask what's needed or suggest a specific change: "How can I make this right?" or "Next time I'll ask before making plans." In a work context: "I'll double-check my emails before sending them in the future. Does that work for you?" When addressing groups, own your impact: "I missed a deadline and let everyone down. Here's how I'm fixing it." This is about demonstrating willingness to change, not just saying the right words.

Sometimes, even with the right approach, the other person isn't ready to reconnect. Maybe they need space or haven't decided how to move forward. Don't pressure for quick forgiveness; instead, say, "I understand if you're not ready to talk. I'm here when you are." This gives them control over the process and shows respect for their feelings.

If tensions linger, check in gently with: "I've been thinking about what happened and want to talk when you're ready." Giving space is sometimes the kindest option; forcing a fix can worsen things. Meanwhile, reflect on what you can improve next time, maybe a reminder or a small ritual to support better communication.

Remember, ruptures don't erase the good in a relationship; they're just bumps along the road. When you consistently work to repair and own your mistakes, trust grows even during tough times, making relationships stronger and more resilient. Over time, these moments become less dramatic and more routine, preventing resentment from building.

Repair varies by context. With partners, focus on vulnerability and emotion: "I snapped last night; you didn't deserve that." At work, be straightforward: "That email was harsher than intended. I apologize." In groups, own your impact and offer solutions: "I missed a deadline and let the group down. Here's my plan to fix it." The approach is consistent and tailors the steps to the situation.

Sometimes, efforts are overlooked or fail to have an impact. The other person may need more time, or the repair may require multiple conversations. Stay available without hovering, letting them know you're open to reconnecting whenever they're ready.

In summary, strong relationships aren't built on flawless communication, but on your ability to repair when things go wrong. Conflict is normal; what matters is your response. Honest ownership of your missteps, without excuses, builds trust and lays the foundation for future connection. Every repair effort strengthens your skills and relationships at home and at work.

Next, we'll explore how emotional intelligence supports group success and fulfillment, translating these skills from individual moments to collective action toward shared goals.

Chapter Seven

Protecting Your Well-Being With Boundaries and Emotional Safety

Saying "No" With Confidence to Overcome the Guilt Trap

Think back to when your phone buzzed with a new request, maybe your boss asked for a "quick favor" that would take up your evening, or a friend invited you out when you just wanted to rest. You hesitated, then said yes, even though your gut said "not today." Later, you felt drained or resentful, questioning why you agreed. If this sounds familiar, you're not alone. Saying no can feel risky if you care about others' feelings or worry about letting people down. Saying no is actually an act of self-respect, not selfishness.

When you say no, you protect time and energy for what matters most. Imagine declining an extra project, not to avoid helping, but because your plate is full. By holding that boundary, you avoid burnout and maintain high quality where it counts. Or say no to a dinner invite when you really need downtime; that isn't cold, it's a way to recharge so you're better for others tomorrow. Research shows that setting healthy boundaries leads to less stress and more satisfaction in relationships and work.

Still, the guilt trap is real. Many of us grew up thinking that saying no is rude or disappointing. Maybe you were praised for being "helpful" or "easygoing," and now feel uneasy prioritizing yourself. Sometimes the fear isn't just about hurting feelings, it's about fearing rejection or missing out. This discomfort often manifests as people-pleasing, the urge to keep everyone happy, even at one's own expense. For some, it's about approval; for others, avoiding conflict or feeling needed. Guilt and obligation can run deep, but they don't have to rule you.

Take a Moment to Think Back in Time

Recall the last time you said yes when you wanted to say no. What came up, fear of disappointing someone, or being seen as difficult? Notice if this happens with certain people or specific words. Write down what you notice, without judgment.

Patterns become clearer once you look for them. You don't have to give long apologies to respect your limits. Warm but direct refusals are powerful: "I appreciate the invite, but I have to pass this time." Or, "I can't take that on right now, but thank you for thinking of me." These statements are direct but kind, no need for debate or over-explaining. If you feel tempted to over-apologize or justify, resist it.

Sometimes, people won't take 'no' the first time. They might insist ("It won't take long!") or guilt-trip ("But we need you!"). Stay calm and repeat yourself: "As I said, I'm not available." It will feel awkward at first, but holding firm respects both your own boundaries and their needs. If you second-guess yourself, remind yourself, "I am allowed to put my needs first." This is self-preservation.

Emotional discomfort after saying no is normal, especially if you face pushback or guilt-tripping. Don't try to argue away your feelings; acknowledge them: "This is uncomfortable because it's new." Sit with the discomfort as it passes and know that every time you honor your boundaries, it gets a bit easier. Remember, it's okay to feel uncomfortable at first. It's a sign that you're stepping out of your comfort zone and asserting your needs, which is a powerful act of self-care.

Saying no confidently is a skill that takes practice. Start small, decline a minor request before moving to bigger ones. Celebrate progress, even if it feels awkward. Over time, saying no feels more freeing. You gain more energy for people and things that matter. People who value you will adjust; some may fall away, and that's okay. Your well-being isn't up for negotiation. Setting boundaries brings a sense of relief, liberating you from the burden of overcommitment and empowering you to focus on what truly matters.

Setting boundaries means drawing necessary lines to keep you healthy and available for what matters most. Saying no with confidence brings you more time, peace, and genuine connection with others and yourself. It's not about shutting people out, but about fostering healthier, more respectful relationships. When you set clear boundaries, you're communicating your needs and expectations, which can lead to a deeper understanding and connection with those around you.

Setting Boundaries at Work Without Alienating Your Team

Work can feel like a constant balancing act. You want to be helpful and collaborative, but you also need to protect your sanity and personal time. Boundaries aren't about shutting people out or being inflexible; they're about protecting your energy and helping everyone work better together. Setting boundaries may make you look selfish or demanding. Still, in reality, clear boundaries at work help teams thrive. When everyone knows what to expect, there's less confusion and resentment. For example, when you start limiting after-hours emails, you signal respect for both your own time and your coworkers'. This reduces burnout and helps the whole team recharge. You could block off your calendar for a couple of hours each morning to focus on deep work, with no meetings or Slack messages, allowing for uninterrupted concentration. That's not just good for you; it benefits everyone by making deadlines easier to meet and reducing last-minute chaos.

People sometimes imagine that boundaries are only needed when things go wrong. Still, they work best when you communicate them up front. Announcing your preferences early, before a crisis, sets the tone for healthy interactions. You could say, "I'll respond to emails during work hours," or "I need quiet time from 9–11 a.m. to really dig into complex projects." These statements are transparent and fair. You're not apologizing; you're simply letting people know how you work best. When others see you modeling this, they often feel relieved and start following suit.

Suppose you're worried about being seen as uncooperative. In that case, it helps to remember that boundaries aren't about avoidance; they serve as a marker of professionalism. Teams function better when everyone has space to concentrate and decompress. Protecting your own time doesn't mean you don't care. It means you want to give your best, not just your leftovers. Most managers and coworkers understand this, especially if you frame it as helping the team achieve more with less stress.

Of course, it's not always smooth sailing. Sometimes, when you set a new boundary, someone tests it, perhaps by continuing to ping you after hours or scheduling meetings during your blocked time. If that happens, address it directly but calmly. For example, if a colleague keeps messaging late at night, respond during work hours with something like, "I appreciate the update! I check messages first thing in the morning and will follow up then." If someone pushes back or acts frustrated, stay steady: "I understand this is urgent, let's talk about how to handle after-hours requests going forward." This approach shifts the conversation toward solutions, rather than blame.

Team norms play a significant role in making boundaries stick. If meetings always run late or get scheduled during lunch breaks, suggest a team discussion about what works for everyone. Perhaps you could agree as a group to have no meetings after 4 p.m., or one "meeting-free" afternoon each week. When boundaries become the norm, not just one person's request, everyone benefits.

Sometimes boundary violations keep happening, even after reminders. At that point, escalate gently but firmly: "I've noticed this keeps coming up. Can we clarify expectations so we're all on the same page?" Keep your language neutral and focused on the goal of smoother teamwork. If necessary, involve a manager or HR, not as a threat, but as a means to obtain support for a healthy work culture.

You might feel anxious before these conversations. That's normal, especially if you've been praised for being "always available." However, boundaries are not just allowed; they're necessary for genuine productivity and respect at work. Over time, people come to appreciate knowing where you stand. They trust your word and understand what they can count on from you.

If you need extra support while setting new limits at work, try journaling the outcomes of each conversation. Notice what works and where you feel resistance, either from others or inside yourself. This reflection turns each experience into a learning opportunity. Celebrate small wins: every time you protect your focus hour or shut down email in the evening without guilt, you reinforce that your needs matter too.

Work boundaries aren't just about saying no, they're about saying yes to working smarter and supporting your team in ways that last. When you set clear limits, you give others permission to do the same, and together you create an environment where everyone can breathe easier and do their best work.

How to Handle Pushback and Old Patterns With Family Boundaries

Family boundaries can feel like walking a tightrope. Even as an adult, old family dynamics often reel you back in. It's tough to set new limits with parents, siblings, or long-term partners because your shared history runs deep. Maybe your mom still expects you to answer every call, or your brother brings up something from years ago to get a rise out of you. Those childhood habits, guilt trips, and rivalry often linger, leading to frustration and guilt when you try to set boundaries.

The challenge is that everyone is used to the old ways. Trying to change the pattern can cause unexpected drama. For example, a parent may guilt you with lines like, "After all I've done for you, you can't even come to dinner?" Siblings might drag up old arguments to hook you into familiar conflicts. Even loving partners sometimes test your resolve by ignoring your new boundaries at first. This pushback is predictable: people resist when routines shift.

Expecting these reactions can help you manage them more effectively. When you set new boundaries, be ready for emotional responses, manipulation, or "testing." If someone says, "So I guess I'm not important to you anymore," that's their discomfort showing, not evidence that your boundary is wrong. The key is to stay steady and clear. You might respond, "I hear you're upset, but this is what I need for my well-being." Show empathy, but don't back down.

Focus on the Present, Not the Past

Breaking old patterns means using language that avoids restarting old arguments. Don't blame or revisit past wounds; focus on what's changed for you. Saying, "I know we've always done things this way, but I'm making some changes for myself," keeps the conversation about your needs and avoids finger-pointing. This isn't about revisiting family history; it's about moving forward in healthier ways. If someone tries to bait you back into old drama, gently bring it back to the present: "I'm focusing on what works for me now."

What If Boundaries Are Ignored?

Sometimes, family members ignore boundaries. Perhaps your dad keeps dropping by unannounced, or your cousin adds you back to a group chat after you've asked them to leave. If your line gets crossed, gently address it: "I noticed my request got overlooked last time. I want to remind you, this is important to me." Stay neutral and avoid unnecessary drama. If your boundaries are repeatedly ignored, consider stepping back to protect your peace.

Taking space isn't cutting people off forever; it's about stepping back until things cool off or people adjust. This could mean muting a chat group or skipping a visit if you're feeling drained. It might feel awkward, but your emotional well-being comes first. Remember, you decide how much access people, including family, have to your time and attention.

Handling Guilt and Resistance

Even after you try, guilt can creep in, and family may sulk. That's normal. It's possible to care about your family and still need space. Remember, boundaries aren't punishments; they are guides for healthy relationships. Change takes time, and families eventually adjust, even if it's slow.

When conversations get tough, use language that feels honest and simple. If someone presses for explanations or wants to argue, keep your answer direct: "This is what I need right now." No long debates necessary; you're not shutting them out, you're making space for healthier relationships for everyone.

Reinforcing New Patterns

Family patterns may be stubborn, but they're not fixed. Each time you set and stick to a boundary, you show others how to treat you. It takes repetition and patience, but each step chips away at old habits, making space for new ones.

If you notice yourself slipping into old roles, the "fixer," "peacemaker," or "reliable one", pause and check in with what you really want in the moment. Boundaries are more complex with family than almost anywhere else. Still, they're also the most powerful way to change your story and build relationships that actually support your well-being.

Emotional Safety Plans for High-Trigger Situations

Certain situations just set you off, sometimes in brutal ways. It could be a tense family gathering where politics arise, or your hands sweat before speaking to a critical boss. These are high-trigger moments when emotions can quickly spiral, leaving you vulnerable. Rather than hoping things will magically improve, it helps to prepare. Emotional safety planning is thinking ahead: recognizing what triggers you, spotting early warning signs, and having clear steps for protecting yourself when things get intense.

Think of emotional safety planning as packing an umbrella when rain threatens. Start by identifying your primary triggers. Is it a specific topic, a person's tone, or crowded rooms? Perhaps your aunt cornering you at holidays, or your boss's sighs at meetings. Once pinpointed, get familiar with your warning signs, maybe tense shoulders, shallow breaths, jaw clenching, or nail-picking. Recognizing these signals early enables you to take action before the situation escalates.

Support is essential. Decide beforehand who you can reach out to, a partner, friend, or group chat, so you have someone who understands when you need help. Sometimes, just having an exit strategy makes all the difference. Know where you can retreat if things get overwhelming: a bathroom, outdoors, or at work, such as taking an errand or making a call in the hallway.

It helps to write down your plan for easy reference. A worksheet could include: "What are my warning signs? Who can I text or call? Where can I take a break?" If you're going to an event with someone close, agree on a "safe word" (like "pineapple") for an immediate rescue or quick exit, no explanation needed.

When you're actually feeling triggered, use simple self-soothing techniques. Excuse yourself, no drama needed: "I need to step out for a few minutes." Sensory tricks work well: feel the floor under your feet, count five things you see, or press your fingers together. Quietly repeat a calming mantra if helpful, such as "I'm safe" or "This will pass." If you can't leave, try closing your eyes briefly and focusing on your breath.

Afterwards, don't rush on as if nothing happened. Take time to let your nervous system reset; this matters as much as having the plan itself. Some people journal about what worked or didn't; others do something enjoyable right after, like a walk, a favorite show, cuddling a pet, or talking to someone who makes them laugh. If it was a rough workday (like after harsh feedback), schedule some self-care, hit the gym, grab tacos with friends, or unwind in your own favorite way.

Making emotional safety planning part of your routine doesn't mean you're always expecting the worst; it just means you're prepared, ready to care for yourself when things get tough. Over time, this gets easier. You'll catch warning signs earlier and handle situations more smoothly. Every small effort adds up, helping keep you safe and steady through challenging moments.

Personalized Emotional Safety Plan Worksheet

Take a few minutes now to sketch out your high-trigger situation plan:

- What are your top three warning signs that overwhelm you?

- Who can you text or call for support?

- Where can you take a short break if needed?

- What's your exit phrase or signal?

- What will you do to recover after the event?

Keep this handy, on your phone, in your bag, on a sticky note in your wallet. When stress rises, you'll have a plan ready to help you stay grounded and safe.

When Others Resist Change, Stay Grounded When You Outgrow Old Roles

Change, even positive change, often stirs things up. Suppose you shift from being quiet to speaking up, or start prioritizing your own well-being after always putting others first. In that case, people notice, and not everyone will immediately applaud you. Friends might tease, saying things like, "Look who's all sensitive now," or "Don't start getting all serious on us." At work, colleagues may make subtle digs or push back when you set boundaries. This resistance is common; it's human nature to cling to the familiar, especially when it means others must adapt their expectations.

People get comfortable with the roles you play, like "peacekeeper" or "the helper." When you change, they may feel unsettled because their expectations are thrown off. It's less about you being difficult and more about them feeling uncomfortable with the shift. Think of it like rearranging furniture in a familiar room. Suddenly, everyone's bumping into things and wants to move them back.

This pushback can trigger old habits, doubting yourself, feeling guilty, or retreating to keep the peace. Staying grounded takes intention. First, recognize what's happening: if someone pushes back, remind yourself,

"My growth may feel threatening to others, and that's okay." This simple reminder helps anchor you. Visualize yourself as a tree, rooted deeply, able to withstand any critical winds.

If doubts creep in, like "Maybe I am making too much of this" or "I should just let it go", pause, breathe, and revisit your reasons for choosing this path. Mindfulness helps; focus on your senses for a moment, or repeat a calming mantra. Minor resets like these break you out of autopilot reactions.

When facing sarcasm or discomfort from others, respond honestly and kindly. You might say, "I get that this feels different, but these changes are important to me," or, "I know it's new for me to speak up more; this matters to me right now." These responses acknowledge others' feelings without abandoning your own. You don't need to convince anyone; state your truth.

If resistance grows stronger, especially from those who benefit from your previous role, consider expanding your support network. Connect with those who value growth: a mentor, a friend who's been through similar changes, or an online group for self-development. Regular check-ins with supportive people can be invaluable; knowing someone "gets it" strengthens your resolve.

If your central circle can't accept your growth and keeps pulling you back, branch out further. Join groups or online communities where you can share your experiences and gain encouragement. Often, connecting with new people who respect your boundaries makes it easier to maintain change in other areas of your life.

As you continue, you'll find others' resistance loses its power. You'll feel less reactive and more centered. Over time, some people will adjust, while others might keep resisting or drift away. That's not yours to fix. What matters is that you stay committed to your growth, even when it's uncomfortable.

Outgrowing old roles opens new doors, relationships shift, deepen, and you attract new people and opportunities. It can feel lonely at first, but the freedom and self-respect you earn make it worthwhile.

Boundaries evolve as you do. Staying grounded during change means holding firm, seeking supportive connections, and reminding yourself why your growth matters. With practice, protecting your well-being becomes natural, even when others wish things would stay the same. Next, we'll explore how emotional intelligence supports group collaboration and helps everyone reach their goals without losing sight of individual needs.

Chapter Eight

Thriving in Uncertainty Under Stress, Change, and Resilience

Stress Mapping to Identify Your Early Warning Signs

S tress is like a phone battery that drains fastest when you need it most. Often, it hides behind a busy schedule or constant notifications. Suddenly shows itself when you snap at someone or forget your keys for the third time. You might think it's just a "bad day," but these are often warning signs from your mind and body that something's off and needs attention. Recognizing these signals early is the key to avoiding meltdowns, harsh words, or sleepless nights filled with racing thoughts. This early recognition gives you the power to take control of your stress, rather than letting it control you.

Spotting stress early gives you the power to act: take a walk, ask for help, or pause and breathe. If ignored, you end up in damage control, apologizing, scrambling to fix errors, or fighting tension headaches. Stress doesn't just feel bad; it seeps into your behavior and body in sneaky ways. Maybe you don't realize your jaw is tight, or you reread the same email repeatedly, or your patience with loved ones vanishes. Stress can also show up as headaches, stomach issues, cravings for junk food, forgetfulness, or zoning out. Skipping meals, snapping at others, or feeling "wired but tired" are all classic signs of distress.

The goal is to recognize your personal "stress signature"; everyone's is a bit different, much like a fingerprint, revealing how you react under pressure. For example, your shoulders tense up or your to-do list feels overwhelming. Your signs could be frequent sighing, teeth grinding, zoning out, becoming extra talkative, or retreating from communication. Other physical cues: neck or back tension, appetite changes, sleep problems, or getting sick more often. Mentally, you might feel scattered, irritable, or unfocused. Emotionally, little things bug you more, and minor mishaps seem huge. Recognizing and understanding these personal stress signatures can make you feel more understood and validated in your experiences.

To find your stress signature, spend a week jotting down moments you feel "off." Don't wait for a meltdown; write down the small stuff, too.

- Did you get a headache after back-to-back meetings?

- Pick a fight after skipping lunch?

- Forget what someone just told you?

Record the situation, your physical and emotional response, and what you did next. Patterns emerge, maybe stress spikes before deadlines or with specific home tasks. Use your phone, a paper journal, or planner; some people prefer color-coding by stress level. What matters most is that you start tracking and noticing these personal trends.

Integrate stress mapping simply into daily life. Set a daily phone reminder to check in with yourself and rate your current stress from 1 (calm) to 10 (maxed out). It takes less than a minute and builds awareness over time. If you prefer, put a sticky note on your fridge or computer with "Stress

Check" as a prompt to scan your body for tension a few times a day. Some people journal about their mood and stress before bed as a personal progress report, helping spot trends before they grow.

Denial is a common obstacle; we often notice stress only when someone else points it out. If you struggle to see your own signs, ask someone close: "Have I seemed more irritable lately?" Trusted friends often notice changes first. Also, watch for repeated patterns: are you always tense before specific meetings or consistently get headaches after family visits? Such patterns hint at building stress behind the scenes.

Build Your Personal Stress Signature Chart

Track your early warning signs for a week using a chart like this:

- **Situation/Trigger** – Monday morning meeting

- **Physical Sign** – clenched jaw, irritable, took deep breaths, running late, racing heart

- **Mental/Emotional Sign** – scattered thinking at spouse

- **What I Did Next** – Skipped lunch, Headache, Short temper, snack, felt better

After a week, review. Do specific triggers keep popping up? Are there any physical signs that appear first? The goal isn't self-criticism, it's catching those first signals early so you can respond before stress takes over.

Stress mapping brings stress into the open, so it stops quietly driving your behavior. Once you know your warning signs, whether it's snacking from overwhelm or turning into a night owl who can't unwind, you can start making minor corrections right away. Catching stress early means you can make adjustments before things spiral out of control.

The Resilience Roadmap of Micro-Habits for Bouncing Back

Resilience isn't a rare trait you're born with; it's built through daily choices and small actions that you repeat, even unconsciously, which help you recover when life throws challenges your way. It's not about being tough all the time or ignoring your feelings; it's about regaining balance and adapting even when things are difficult. The good news is, anyone can develop resilience with simple, manageable habits that fit seamlessly into your daily life. These habits are the key to a more hopeful outlook, even in the face of stress and challenges.

You don't need long stretches of free time or a special retreat to start. Think of resilience as your emotional immune system, strengthened by easy routines you can stick with. For busy people, "micro-habits" are the key, quick, practical actions that fit seamlessly into your daily life and add up over time. These habits might seem trivial, but their power lies in being sustainable and repeatable. For instance, each morning, while brushing your teeth or making coffee, ask yourself, "What's one thing I'm looking forward to today?" Even on tough days, there's usually something: a hot drink, a favorite podcast, or just a quiet moment before the day begins. This quick check-in gently prompts your brain to notice the positives, however small.

At night, try a brief reflection: name one thing that went right today, no matter how minor. You can easily find a parking spot or have a genuine conversation with a coworker. Small as they seem, these moments matter. They help prevent your mind from getting stuck on stress, reminding you that good things also happen. Want to go further? Do a weekly gratitude scan, and list three things you appreciated this week. It doesn't need to be profound; perhaps "leftover pizza" or "my dog's snoring" makes the list. Over time, this habit retrains your focus away from what's missing toward what's sustaining you.

Another powerful micro-habit is "micro-support." Once a day or week, send a quick check-in text to someone you care about. A simple "Thinking of you!" or "How are you today?" can brighten their day and remind you of the importance of connection in building resilience.

The best way to make these habits stick is to pair them with routines you already have, what habit experts call "habit-pairing." Attach your morning check-in to your coffee routine or commute. Reflect on what went well while getting ready for bed or shutting down your laptop. Practice gratitude on Friday afternoon before the weekend begins. The less you have to remember, the easier it becomes to maintain these habits.

Visual reminders also help. Track your micro-habits using an app, a hand-drawn chart, or stickers. Some keep charts inside a cabinet or on the fridge, others set calendar reminders. Watching your streaks build can keep you motivated, and missing a day is no big deal; start again the next day.

Celebrating progress matters. Share your small wins with a friend or group who understands your journey. You might text each other weekly successes or motivate each other to find new gratitude items. This kind of encouragement boosts your accountability and reminds you you're not alone in building resilience.

Your Micro-Habit Menu

Choose any two habits below to try this week. Write them on sticky notes and place them where you'll see them, on the bathroom mirror, coffee maker, or car dashboard.

- **Morning check-in:** "What am I looking forward to?"

- **End-of-day reflection:** "What went right today?"

- **Weekly gratitude scan:** "Three things I appreciated."

- **Micro-support:** "Text someone a kind word."

Test various combinations to find what suits your routine and personality. Adjust as needed; there's no single right way to build resilience. With time, these micro-habits become automatic, like buckling your seatbelt or locking the door.

You're building muscle memory for bouncing back, one small step at a time.

Scripts for Navigating Transitions to Cope With Major Life Changes

Significant changes can feel like sudden storms; one day, life feels predictable, the next, everything is upended. Losing a job disrupts not just your routine but your sense of self. Breakups and divorces bring mixed emotions, relief, sadness, anger, and confusion. Moving, especially involuntarily, can make you feel unmoored. Illness, whether your own or a loved one's, forces you to adapt and ask for help in uncomfortable ways. Transitions don't just change your external world; they stir up a whirlwind of inner emotions. Feeling one way one day, and the opposite the next, is normal.

Having a roadmap makes these emotional rollercoasters easier. The "Acknowledge, Accept, Act, Adjust" framework breaks down the chaos:

- **Acknowledge:** Recognize the loss or change, even if it's positive. Naming your feelings gives you some control over them.

- **Accept:** Allow your emotions without judging them. You can be angry about moving or scared about being single, even if the change improves things. Acceptance means letting feelings surface without self-criticism.

- **Act:** Take a small step forward, whether it's making a list or telling someone you aren't okay. Reaching out for support, even with a simple text, opens the door to connection.

- **Adjust:** Gradually find your new normal through patience and experimentation. You may need to tweak routines or ask for help more than once.

Communicating During Transitions

It can feel awkward to talk about significant changes. People may not know what to say, and you might worry about burdening them. Be direct: "I'm going through a tough time and may be less available than usual." This sets expectations without oversharing. If you need support, spell it out: "Can you check in on me this week?" Most people want to help, but need guidance from you.

At work or with acquaintances, stay professional but honest: "I appreciate your patience as I adjust." If someone tries to fix things but you want them to listen, gently redirect: "Thank you for caring. Right now, I need someone to listen." This protects your emotional energy.

Managing Guilt and Setting Boundaries

You may feel guilty asking for help, especially if you're usually the strong one. Remember, needing support is not a weakness; everyone faces hard times, and letting others step up gives them a chance to give back. If you fear being a burden, think of times you've supported others; people genuinely want to do the same for you.

Some people, uncomfortable with your new reality, may try to rush your recovery or dismiss your struggle. They may say things like, "Just stay positive!" Set boundaries kindly, such as: "I appreciate your intentions, but I need space to feel what I'm feeling." This is how you protect yourself without alienating others.

If someone continues to drain your energy or ignore your needs, be clear: "I'm focusing on my own needs right now and may not be as available." Though it feels awkward, prioritizing your wellbeing allows you to move through change with less resentment and more self-respect.

Creating Routines and Finding Your Way

As you carve out new routines, replacing an old commute with morning walks or scheduling regular calls with distant friends, give yourself permission to experiment. Some things will help, others won't; progress isn't linear, and setbacks are normal. Each honest conversation, each moment you forgive yourself for not having it all together, is real growth.

Major life transitions are challenging but revealing. You discover strengths and support systems you never expected to find. Through honest communication and clear boundaries, you lighten your emotional load. Even amidst the mess, you find resilience, and sometimes, your hardest chapters become your most transformative.

Quick Wins for Overwhelmed Schedules to Prevent Burnout

Burnout sneaks in quietly, but its effects are anything but subtle. Unlike regular stress, which flares up and then dies down after a deadline or a tough week, burnout is a slow, draining leak that leaves you feeling hollow. You might wonder if you're tired or need a vacation. Still, if exhaustion lingers day after day and you wake up dreading things you once enjoyed, something deeper is going on. Burnout is more than being busy or stressed; it's the feeling that you're running on fumes, your motivation has given up, and you're just going through the motions. Classic signs of burnout include chronic exhaustion (not just sleepiness, but bone-deep tiredness that rest doesn't alleviate), a creeping sense of cynicism or detachment (perhaps you're rolling your eyes more, or snapping at work drama you used to tolerate), and a noticeable decline in your performance. You might feel "checked out," like you're watching your life from the outside, not really participating. Suddenly, the things that used to light you up now feel heavy or pointless.

Everyone has different risk factors for burnout, so finding your personal weak spots is essential. Consider your current routine: Where do you feel the most exhausted? Is it an endless email chain at work, a never-shrinking list of family obligations, or the emotional load of supporting everyone else? It could be the pressure to always say yes, even when you're maxed out. Are you skipping sleep to get more done, or bringing your phone to bed and scrolling through work messages at midnight? It's easy to lose sight of your limits if boundaries blur or you don't have time for recovery. Ask yourself: "What tasks drain me most?" or "Where do I feel least supported?" Sometimes, the most exhausting thing isn't even physical; it's the feeling that nobody notices how much you're carrying.

When burnout is circling, quick wins matter. You don't need an elaborate plan; even five minutes can make a difference. Try a power nap for 15–20 minutes, not long enough to feel groggy, just enough to reboot your brain. If napping isn't practical, stand up and stretch for a five-minute movement break: walk around the block, roll your shoulders, or do a few jumping jacks in the kitchen. These tiny bursts of movement clear mental cobwebs fast. Protect your lunch break from meetings whenever possible; a real pause in your day keeps exhaustion from piling up. Even two minutes of desk meditation can reset your mood. Close your eyes, breathe deeply, and focus on the sensation of air moving in and out. No fancy skills required. The point isn't to escape problems but to give yourself mini "reset" buttons so stress doesn't keep stacking up.

Long-term burnout prevention relies on establishing non-negotiable rituals for recovery, setting tiny boundaries that protect your energy before it's depleted. Designate one evening per week as a no-work zone. Turn off email notifications, silence your phone, and tell family or roommates this is your recharge time. Rituals give structure to self-care; it's cooking without distractions, reading in bed, or taking a long shower after everyone else is asleep. Don't wait until you're desperate; schedule these breaks like any other important meeting. If guilt creeps in for protecting time or saying no, remind yourself that burned-out people aren't helpful to anyone.

Another effective strategy is the "burnout buddy" system: pick someone, a friend, partner, or coworker, and agree to check in with each other regularly about stress levels and boundaries. Sometimes just having someone ask "How are you doing, really?" makes it easier to be honest about needing a break or shifting priorities. This isn't about venting endlessly; it's mutual support and gentle accountability.

Burnout doesn't always announce itself with flashing lights. Sometimes it shows up as boredom, forgetting appointments, or losing interest in things that once mattered to you. If you catch yourself wishing the week away or feeling numb more than not, listen to those signals. Swap one draining task for something that refreshes you, even if it's only for a few minutes. The smallest reset, stepping outside for fresh air or saying "no" to one extra request, can start to turn things around. No one is immune to burnout, but everyone can take steps to reduce its grip with quick wins and protective routines that fit the chaos of real life.

Reframing Failure as Feedback to Turn Setbacks Into Growth

Nobody avoids all setbacks. Mistakes and failures are part of pursuing anything meaningful. Still, it's easy to forget this in the moment. Many admire high achievers and assume they never stumble, but that's misleading. J.K. Rowling, for example, faced many rejections before Harry Potter's success; each one felt personal, but she learned from feedback, adjusted her work, and tried again. What appeared as endless failure became the base of her achievements. Athletes and leaders make public mistakes, too, but what sets them apart is their ability to use setbacks as learning opportunities.

To normalize setbacks, it helps to remove the shame often associated with them. Failure doesn't mean you're incapable; it means you took a risk and stretched beyond your comfort zone. Rarely failing usually means you aren't pushing yourself. Every mistake offers a lesson if you pause to reflect. The key is to analyze what happened objectively, without self-criticism or denial. That's where a "failure debrief" helps, breaking down the experience so it works for you.

Start by reviewing what happened, as objectively as possible. Did you botch a presentation, miss a deadline, lose your cool, or see a project flop? Next, distinguish what you truly controlled from external factors. Did you prepare enough? Was the timing unlucky? This step keeps you from unfairly blaming yourself and highlights areas you can influence next time. Finally, consider: What's one or two things you could try differently next time? Focus on small, practical changes rather than overhauling everything. For example, ask for feedback sooner or rehearse with a friend before your next presentation.

Talking about failure can feel vulnerable. Using prepared phrases can help. Rather than ignoring disappointment or pretending nothing went wrong, try: "This didn't go as planned, but here's what I learned." Or, to be kinder to yourself: "I'm proud I tried, even if it was tough." These simple shifts help focus on learning rather than shame, and let others support you.

Setbacks often linger in your mind, causing rumination and shame long after the event. Breaking this cycle is vital for growth. One tactic is to write a letter to your future self, detail the setback, and outline what you'll do differently next time. This processes your emotions and gives you a plan for the future.

Another helpful strategy is the 24-hour "feel it, then frame it" rule. When things go wrong, let yourself experience whatever you're feeling: anger, disappointment, embarrassment, for a day. Don't force yourself to look for the silver lining immediately. After 24 hours, intentionally shift perspectives: What did you learn? What's the next step? This allows room for emotion, but doesn't let it take over.

Stepping out of negative loops also means managing your self-talk. If you catch yourself thinking, "I always mess up" or "I'll never succeed," challenge it with a more balanced statement: "This was tough, but I've handled hard things before." If regrets linger, remind yourself that setbacks are an essential part of any worthwhile growth story.

Growth-minded individuals don't avoid failure; they use it as an opportunity for self-improvement. The difference between a dead end and a detour is how you respond. Give both yourself and others space to be imperfect, and you'll feel freer to take healthy risks.

In summary, setbacks are invitations to adapt, not reasons to quit. Each time you learn from what didn't work and try again with new insight, you build both resilience and confidence. These skills benefit all areas of life, work, relationships, and teamwork, and can lead to faster, more harmonious progress.

Remember, emotional intelligence isn't just about recognizing emotions or managing stress; it's also about turning adversity into an opportunity for growth. In the next section, we'll see how these skills translate into better teamwork and collective achievement, because growth happens together, and every big goal is accomplished with others.

Chapter Nine

Professional Growth and Team Success by Using EQ at Work

Scripts to Build Confidence for Speaking Up in Meetings

There's a moment in nearly every meeting when you feel a spark, an idea or question, but second-guess yourself. You replay the last time you spoke and were cut off or dismissed, or you hear your inner critic whisper, "What if you sound clueless?" If you've left meetings frustrated that you stayed silent, you're not alone. This tension between wanting to contribute and worrying about how it'll land is real, even for seasoned professionals. Imposter syndrome and past negative experiences, like being shut down or ignored, naturally make you hesitate.

Anxiety about speaking up isn't limited to big presentations. Everyday scenarios, sharing an opinion in front of leadership, challenging a decision, or trying to join a quick-moving discussion, can trigger self-doubt. You may worry about interrupting, being seen as pushy, or having your ideas brushed aside. These barriers affect everyone, not just introverts. Even confident people can freeze at times, ironically, when their voice is most needed.

Micro-preparation routines help build confidence before meetings. Many people steady their nerves with a few deep breaths in private or practice a power pose before entering. The goal isn't to feel fearless, but to calm your body so your mind can work effectively. Repeat to yourself, "I have something valuable to contribute." This isn't just affirmation, it's a reminder that your perspective matters, regardless of your role. Another quick trick: plant both feet, open your posture, inhale slowly through your nose, and exhale through your mouth. This simple action can steady nerves.

Power poses, like the Wonder Woman stance (hands on hips, shoulders back for a minute or two), may feel silly at first. Still, research shows they boost confidence hormones and reduce stress. Do this off-camera before a virtual meeting or in a private spot. These rituals signal to your nervous system: I'm ready.

Go-to scripts help when it's time to contribute.

- To build on others' ideas, say, "I'd like to add to what was said earlier about [topic]..." or "I want to build on [Name] 's point with another angle."

- To challenge respectfully: "I see it a bit differently. Can I offer another perspective?"

- To raise a concern without sounding confrontational: "I have a question about how this decision will affect our team."

These are not magic passwords, but they give you a launchpad instead of fumbling for words.

If your mind goes blank or you're interrupted, don't retreat into silence. If cut off, say, "I'd like to finish my point before we move on." This is direct yet fair. If you lose your train of thought, pause and say, "Let me take a moment to gather my thoughts." Most people focus on their own contributions and won't fixate on your pauses.

A Quick-Start Confidence Checklist

- **Before every meeting:**

  - Write down one thing you want to say (even just a question).

  - Remind yourself: "My input matters."

  - Take three deep breaths or do a power pose.

- **In the meeting:**

  - Use a starter script when contributing.

  - If interrupted: "I'd like to finish my thought before we move on."

  - If you lose your place: "Let me take a moment to gather my thoughts."

- **Afterward:**

  - Jot down what went well and note what to try next time.

Building confidence isn't about eliminating fear, but acting alongside it. Each time you speak up, even nervously, you prove your fears wrong. The more you use these routines and scripts, the easier it becomes for your authentic voice to shine through.

EQ for Meetings, Slack, and Email to Read the Room

Today's workplaces often involve toggling between virtual and in-person settings, Zoom, Slack, emails, and hybrid offices. Emotional intelligence

(EQ) now requires recognizing subtle, less visible signals. It's not just about reading faces; you need to detect clues when people go silent on chat, keep cameras off, or send brief, unemotional emails. Silence after a message in Slack can be just as telling as body language in a boardroom. An update that gets no reaction leaves you unsure if your idea was appreciated or ignored.

Decoding these cues relies on observation and intuition. In person, you notice side glances, crossed arms, or someone sighing, a sign of frustration. Virtually, responses can be trickier: a camera may switch off after a tense moment, only emojis respond to your chat, or a participant never reacts at all. Reading the room starts by noticing who speaks and who remains quiet. Are a few dominating while others pull back? Are people sticking to safe, scripted comments? Tone matters: voices may sound tense, flat, or forced, or participants might answer quickly to move the meeting along.

Micro-expressions and digital signals also reveal a lot. In person, you might see an eye roll or someone biting their lip during a tricky topic. On video calls, someone may fidget, mute frequently, or look away to type. Chat channels hold clues too: a flood of thumbs-up emojis could hide disagreement; silence may mean confusion or disengagement. Even email holds signals, a blunt "Noted." without a sign-off can feel cold; a sudden switch to formality may suggest tension.

Watch for changes in pace or topic. If the discussion speeds up, people might want to escape discomfort. When the group dwells on small details or circles the same issue, unspoken tension could be present. Noticing these patterns, whether in meetings or chats, can alert you to problems. If a typically vocal colleague falls silent or if conversations become chaotic, pause to reassess.

When you sense awkwardness or tension, name it gently so people feel included without being singled out. Say, "I'm sensing some hesitation, any concerns to address?" This approach welcomes honesty. Or, "I noticed fewer people are chiming in, let's do a quick check-in," which invites quieter folks to share. Often, acknowledging the tension eases it, making the group more comfortable.

Digital EQ is unique. Emails and chats can miscommunicate tone; what reads as clear to one may seem cold or harsh to another. Before sending, double-check your tone: read it out loud or imagine receiving it after a long day. Friendly sign-offs like "Thanks for your input!" or "Looking forward to your thoughts" help keep feedback positive and show you value your colleagues' voices. If you receive a brief or cryptic message ("Not sure about this"), don't react defensively. Clarify: "Could you say more about your concerns? I want to make sure I understand."

Emojis can help set a warm tone, but use them in moderation and tailor your approach to your audience. If uncertain how your words might land, pause and reconsider. Often, someone's chilly response isn't personal; they may just be distracted or tired.

Digital Room Reading

Recall a recent remote meeting or Slack chat where you felt confused or uneasy. What signals tipped you off? Who didn't speak? Did the conversation feel rushed? Note three things you observed and one way you might check in next time, by posing an open-ended question or suggesting a one-on-one to clear the air.

The more you sharpen your awareness of subtle signals, online and in person, the better you'll become at guiding conversations toward openness and understanding. EQ now extends to every ping, post, and pause throughout your workday, not just face-to-face exchanges.

Navigating Office Politics With Integrity

Office politics often evokes discomfort, reminding us of whispered hallway conversations, circulating rumors, or the subtle push to maintain favor. Yet, it isn't just about manipulation; from an emotional intelligence perspective, it's about understanding informal power dynamics and how relationships drive outcomes. Every workplace has unwritten rules. Decisions may be made after meetings or influenced by the actions of particular individuals, regardless of official channels or job titles. Recognizing these dynamics isn't about becoming manipulative; it's about understanding them. Still, about understanding how things actually get done, so you can engage with clarity and integrity.

Specific projects succeed only because of key backing or because particular colleagues wield influence that surpasses their roles. You may notice subtle alliances, such as those formed through socializing together or gaining inside information early. These cues show how influence actually operates. It's not wrong to notice them, nor is it "dirty" to use this awareness to build sincere relationships. The distinction is in your intent: use what you see to foster trust and do valuable work, rather than merely advance yourself.

Staying true to yourself isn't easy amid constant pressure to "play the game." It helps to ground yourself in personal principles for when situations get murky. A simple guiding question: Does this action align with my values? If you don't want your words or choices publicized, that's a sign to pause. Sometimes, people will try to involve you in venting sessions about others; you don't need to participate. Listen briefly, but then redirect: "I prefer to focus on solutions, not blame." If drawn into giving an opinion about a colleague's performance or ideas, check your own motives: Will this help the team, or just fuel drama? If it feels questionable, hold back.

When discussions slip into gossip or backchannels, protect your boundaries without escalating. Saying, "I'm not comfortable discussing this without them present," sets a respectful limit. This is especially helpful if prompted to criticize a colleague in their absence or pulled into disputes. You can also shift the focus with "Let's talk about ways to move forward," keeping the discussion constructive.

Diplomacy is essential. If asked to join in drama or exclude a teammate, remain neutral but transparent: "I want to support the team's goals, not pick sides." If this upsets someone, restore trust directly: "I respect your perspective, and my intention is always to support what's best for our group." This communicates you're focused on collective outcomes rather than personal alliances.

Occasionally, you'll be caught in the middle, perhaps between clashing coworkers or with leadership expecting quiet support for controversial choices. Don't deny the discomfort. Acknowledge it and honestly: "I see both sides and want us all to find common ground." If someone's disappointed you didn't offer complete support, avoid defensiveness. Refocus on shared goals: "I care about our working relationship and want us both to succeed."

At times, you might feel excluded for not conforming to group expectations, left out of conversations or projects. Instead of withdrawing or retaliating, address it respectfully: "I noticed I wasn't included on that project. Could we talk about how I can stay involved moving forward?" Presenting your request collaboratively fosters dialogue rather than confrontation.

Values-Based Choices in Office Politics

- Does this action align with my values?

- Is this if everyone involved were present?

- Does this comment solve problems or create conflict?

- Am I building or undermining trust?

- Will I feel good about this decision tomorrow?

Navigating office politics with emotional intelligence involves recognizing power dynamics and staying true to your values. By prioritizing honest communication and principled choices, you protect both your reputation and peace of mind, even in challenging environments.

Coaching, Feedback Loops, and Team Resilience to Lead With EQ

When you lead a team with emotional intelligence, you see shifts that ripple through every project and conversation. People relax and share fundamental ideas. Mistakes get addressed without blame or panic. You notice that your team recovers from setbacks quickly, almost like they have an invisible net beneath them. There's less drama, more trust, and a kind of energy that fuels collaboration instead of draining it. This is psychological safety in action. It doesn't just feel nice; it drives results. Teams led with EQ show lower turnover and higher engagement. People actually want to come to work, and they stick around longer because they trust the environment.

EQ-driven leadership changes the dynamic from "command and control" to "coach and empower." Instead of barking orders or micromanaging, you start guiding people to find their own solutions. You might use coaching frameworks, such as the **GROW** model (**G**oal, **R**eality, **O**ptions, **W**ill), tailored for emotional growth. Let's say a team member is struggling. Start with:

- **Goal:** "What's your goal with this project?" You're helping them to clarify what they want, not what you assume they want.

- **Reality:** "What's happening now?" You give them space to talk about obstacles, maybe it's workload, or it's fear of conflict with a peer.

- **Options:** "What could you try differently?" This might spark creative thinking or reveal hidden strengths.

- **Will:** "What support do you need to move forward?" or "What's one step you'll commit to this week?" These questions aren't just about work; they make it safe for someone to admit uncertainty or ask for help.

Coaching also means tuning into feelings, not just facts. It's common to ask, "How did that situation make you feel?" or "What was hardest for you in this process?" These questions might sound soft at first, but they open dialogue and build trust. When someone feels seen emotionally, they'll be more honest about what's working and what's not. That honesty leads to better decisions and fewer costly surprises down the road.

Feedback loops are the backbone of resilient teams. Instead of saving feedback for annual reviews or never saying a word until something goes wrong, you create regular rituals. Maybe your team does retrospectives after big projects or even short "after-action" reviews at the end of each week. The focus isn't just on deliverables but on the emotional climate: What felt smooth? Where did tension pop up? Who seemed checked out? For example, you might ask during a debrief, "How did everyone feel about the pace of this sprint?" or "Were there moments where we missed each other emotionally?" This isn't fluff; it's where teams identify patterns before they become problems. Over time, these habits make continuous improvement feel normal instead of threatening.

You can build these habits with simple scripts and rituals. Start meetings with a quick check-in: "Let's go around and share one word for how we're feeling." This takes less than a minute but creates an immediate connection. Others use a "feelings round" at the end of meetings, where everyone shares a word or short phrase about how they're feeling as they leave the room. These rituals surface tension without confrontation and allow space for both positive and negative emotions. If someone says, "Overwhelmed," that's a flag to pause and check if support or clarification is needed.

Tough conversations get easier when you approach them with EQ tools. If a project went off the rails, avoid finger-pointing and instead ask, "What have we learned emotionally as a team from this project?" This reframes mistakes as growth opportunities instead of failures. It also gives quieter voices permission to speak up about stressors or miscommunications that may have been brushed aside before.

Celebrating wins as a group also matters for resilience. Don't just recognize outcomes, highlight emotional skills displayed by the team: "I appreciated how we stayed calm during that last-minute change," or "I noticed how well our group supported each other when things got tough." These moments reinforce that emotional effort is valued alongside technical skills.

If you're new to leading with EQ or coaching frameworks like GROW, start small. Try weaving one new question or ritual into your next team meeting. Experiment with feedback loops by asking for input after a mini-project: "What worked well? What would we change next time?" Notice how people respond when you show curiosity about their feelings as well as their results.

Adapt these ideas to your culture; there's no single right way to lead with EQ, but the common thread is genuine care for both people and progress. When teams trust that their emotions matter, not just their output, they become more adaptable, creative, and able to weather whatever changes come their way.

Use EQ for Every Work Relationship to Manage Up, Down, and Across

Work relationships vary in direction, each drawing on emotional intelligence (EQ) differently.

- **Managing up** involves interacting with those holding power over your work, growth, and job security. It's more than impressing your boss; it's about honest communication, seeking support, and handling tough feedback. For instance, if your manager mainly criticizes and rarely praises, EQ helps you process critique constructively and communicate your needs confidently, perhaps by saying, "I'd appreciate your perspective on this challenge." This signals respect and openness without sacrificing confidence.

- **Managing down** reverses the authority dynamic. Now, you must motivate direct reports who may feel burnt out or disengaged.

If someone is missing deadlines or losing enthusiasm, rather than defaulting to reprimands, foster a connection by asking, "How can I support you better?" This approach invites honest conversation, helping you discover root issues, whether they're personal challenges or unclear expectations. EQ here means listening for unspoken issues and showing genuine investment in your team's success.

- **Managing across** covers interactions with peers and colleagues who are neither above nor below you hierarchically. Power is replaced by influence, and EQ becomes crucial when working alongside competitive or territorial peers. In these situations, keep the focus on cooperation by saying, "Let's clarify our shared goals." This shifts attention to mutual objectives and defuses turf battles. Demonstrate curiosity by asking questions and remain patient when disagreements arise or progress stalls.

Trust and credibility are essential in all these relationships. Reliability, consistently following through on commitments, builds trust. If you promise a status update by Friday, deliver it early. Transparency is just as vital: admit mistakes without shifting blame. For example, if you miscalculate a budget, say, "I missed that update. Let me fix it now." People don't expect perfection; they value accountability and a willingness to make things right.

Emotional maturity also means navigating difficult situations fairly and calmly. If your boss begins to micromanage, react constructively: "I'd like to revisit expectations so we're both on the same page." This invites clarity and resets boundaries without confrontation. When a direct report resists feedback or deadlines, avoid power struggles and encourage dialogue by saying, "Let's talk about what's getting in the way, what would help you move forward?" This communicates care for their perspective as well as the results.

Peer conflicts can be uniquely challenging. If disputes recur or collaboration stalls, it's reasonable to seek help. Propose mediation or involve a third party if direct resolution isn't working. Address ongoing tension neutrally: "I notice we've had some friction lately. Can we talk about what's going on and find a better way to work together?" Involving HR or a trusted manager is a sign of valuing effective teamwork, not failure.

In all these relationships, EQ is critical. Use it to listen fully, ask thoughtful questions, and maintain composure in tense moments. Following through on commitments and owning up to mistakes builds trust, even if it goes unacknowledged. These habits create a culture of trust upwards, downwards, and sideways.

Ultimately, emotional intelligence is foundational; it extends beyond meetings and reviews into every work interaction. Whether you're helping a struggling teammate, handling tough feedback from above, or resolving peer conflict, EQ provides the clarity and connection vital to success. Next, we'll explore weaving these skills into daily routines until they become second nature, at work, at home, and everywhere else.

Chapter Ten

Integrating Emotional Intelligence Into Daily Life

The 30-Day EQ Challenge of Daily Micro-Actions for Real Change

E veryday moments, such as standing in a grocery line and feeling irritation rise, offer real opportunities to practice emotional intelligence (EQ). It's not about grand gestures but in small, repeated choices: pausing before reacting, noticing another's tone, staying aware of your own mood shifts. If you want to build genuine EQ skills without disrupting your routine or investing hours in self-help, rest assured, you're in the right place. The 30-Day EQ Challenge is designed to be simple and easy to follow, making it a confident choice for your personal growth journey.

Lasting change comes from micro-habits: small, regular actions that are easy to stick with and, over time, quietly rewire your emotional habits. Trying to change overnight rarely works, but a single small step each day can take you much farther than you expect. The 30-Day EQ Challenge is not just a series of tasks; it's a transformative journey that can inspire and motivate you to become the best version of yourself.

The 30-Day EQ Challenge is built around daily mini-tasks, all five minutes or less, that boost every aspect of EQ: self-awareness, regulation, empathy, boundaries, and communication. Each day is a low-pressure opportunity to practice real-world skills. Some days call for noticing and reflecting, others for small acts or new conversations. The point isn't perfection, but progress. By focusing on progress, you can feel encouraged and less pressured, making the journey more enjoyable and rewarding.

You'll start with self-awareness, progress to regulation, then empathy, boundaries, and finally communication. By month's end, you'll have practiced, not just read about, EQ, in all its dimensions. With enough daily variety, you won't get bored; tasks rotate from solo check-ins and spirited reflection to honest chats and playful experiments.

Your 30-Day Challenge Tracker

Days 1–7: Building Self-Awareness

Start by noticing your emotional landscape.

- **Day 1**: Write down three emotions you have experienced and their sources. Identifying your feelings brings clarity and reveals patterns.

- **Day 2**: Focus on a specific physical signal of emotion, such as a tight jaw or a fluttery stomach, and record it.

- **Day 3**: Utilize a feelings wheel (which can be found online by searching "feelings wheel") to accurately label a complex emotion.

- **Day 4**: Take a moment at midday for a one-minute self-check-in. Ask yourself, "How am I feeling right now?" Without trying to change anything, notice your feelings.

- **Day 5**: Take a mindful pause before responding in conversation. When you feel triggered, count to three and take a deep breath before speaking. This simple act helps interrupt reactive cycles.

- **Days 6 and 7:** To increase awareness, try briefly journaling about a recurring frustration. Identify any patterns you notice. Additionally, track your mood in the morning, afternoon, and evening to see how it shifts throughout the day. Mood-tracking apps can be helpful for this. Over time, these small practices will create a map of your

Days 8–14: Regulating Emotions and Taking Small Actions

Now, put awareness into action.

- **Day 8**: Calmly label an intense emotion as it arises; simply naming stress can lessen its grip.

- **Day 9**: When you feel tension rising, take a moment to pause and breathe deeply for five breaths or for one minute.

- **Day 10**: Use the "I feel" formula ("I feel _____ when _____ because _____") for a low-stakes issue to build comfort with truthful and transparent expression.

- **Day 11**: Take five minutes to have a conversation with someone, giving them your full attention without any distractions from your phone.

- **Day 12**: When feeling stressed, comfort yourself by placing your hand on your chest and repeating a calming phrase: "This is tough, but temporary."

- **Day 13**: Write down one positive thing that happened today, no matter how small.

- **Day 14**: Take a moment to reflect on the most significant emotional victory you experienced this week. Consider what factors contributed to making that win possible.

Days 15–21: Empathy and Boundaries

Week three focuses on relationships.

- **Day 15**: Establish and maintain a clear boundary, such as declining an additional task or requesting an hour without interruptions; pay attention to how it feels. Boundaries are not barriers; they are healthy limits.

- **Day 16**: Observe two people interacting (live or on TV) and interpret their feelings by analyzing body language and tone, thereby enhancing your empathy.

- **Day 17**: Ask someone an open-ended question and listen without interrupting, resisting the urge to offer advice or share personal stories.

- **Day 18**: Recall a time when someone deeply empathized with you. What actions did they take? How did their support help you? Reflect on how you can offer similar empathy to others.

- **Day 19**: Practice gentle honesty by expressing how someone's actions made you feel, without blaming them. For example, "I felt hurt when plans changed at the last minute because I was looking forward to seeing you."

- **Day 20**: Listen supportively to someone while withholding solutions; simple affirmations, such as "That sounds hard," or "I'm here if you want to talk," are sufficient. The goal is to be present, not to solve problems.

- **Day 21**: Take time to restore yourself after demanding

interactions. Engage in a walk, listen to music, have a snack, or rest. Practicing self-care replenishes your emotional energy.

Days 22–30: Communication Skills and Real-World Practice

Put EQ into live action.

- **Day 22**: Count how often you interrupt in conversation, even mentally; try to listen fully, allowing others to complete their thoughts.

- **Day 23**: Give positive feedback using **SBIR** (**S**ituation, **B**ehavior, **I**mpact, **R**esponse). "During yesterday's meeting, when you clarified the following steps, it made me feel organized. Thank you!"

- **Day 24**: Ask a colleague or friend for feedback and invite them to suggest one idea for how you could improve.

- **Day 25**: Apply **SBIR** to constructive feedback about a small matter (On our call [situation], when my point was cut off [behavior], I felt unheard [impact]. Could we make sure everyone gets time? [response]). This honors clarity, not conflict.

- **Day 26**: When a disagreement occurs, take a moment to observe your initial reaction. Pause deliberately before escalating the situation or defending your position.

- **Day 27**: Revisit an old emotional habit, such as people-pleasing or shutting down, and choose one small way to act differently.

- **Day 28**: List three ways you've changed since starting. Recognizing progress, no matter how small, fuels motivation.

- **Day 29**: Celebrate and treat yourself for consistently showing up, even if it's not perfect.

- **Day 30**: Share something you've learned about your emotional intelligence or yourself with someone, or online if you'd like.

It's not about perfect attendance or flawless EQ; it's about repeatedly showing interest in your emotional growth. If you miss a day, resume, the brain learns best through steady, consistent effort. The tracker, calendar, or digital lets you see, at a glance, a growing record of your progress.

Your EQ Challenge Experience

After each week, pause for a five-minute reflection: What surprised you? What felt easier or tougher than expected? Did others respond differently when you listened better or set more precise boundaries? Keep these notes brief. Even short reflections help reveal growth areas and recurring patterns.

Each of these thirty days is a seed for self-awareness, steadier reactions, more authentic relationships, and quicker progress toward both personal and professional goals.

What to Do When Old Patterns Return

If you've been making progress with emotional intelligence only to get tripped up by old habits, like snapping at a partner, shutting down, or reverting to people-pleasing, you're not alone. No one rewires years of emotional patterns without setbacks. Sometimes, you can feel calm and self-aware, only to suddenly slip back into old behaviors. These moments don't erase your progress. Relapses are a regular part of growth; emotional habits form over years, shaped by family, stress, and environment. When you're tired or stressed, your brain conserves energy by reverting to what's familiar. Recognize that setbacks are signals to pause and recalibrate, not evidence of failure.

When you notice an old pattern, name it, aloud or silently. This could be as simple as acknowledging, "I'm getting defensive again," or "I'm avoiding this conversation." Naming disrupts autopilot responses and creates a moment to choose differently. Next, take a mindful breath or step away briefly, walk to another room, get some water, or close your eyes and ground yourself. These small pauses interrupt the momentum of the old habit and help your brain align with your intentions.

After the pause, ask yourself: "What do I need right now?" Go beyond the immediate reaction to uncover underlying needs, reassurance, control, validation, or space. Asking this question gives you a chance to shift your automatic response; you don't have to fix everything at once. It's about giving yourself a window to try something new.

Then, take one small, different action. If you shut down during conflict, say, "I need a minute to think" instead of going silent. If you default to fixing others' problems, offer empathy instead: "That sounds hard." If you get loud, try an "I feel" statement: "I'm frustrated because I don't feel heard." Even if it feels awkward, these intentional steps interrupt old patterns and strengthen new ones; each small choice counts, even if you only manage it sometimes.

When communicating about slips with others, honesty is better than perfection. If you snap or shut down, own it as soon as possible: "I just fell into my old habit, can I try again?" This invites repair rather than defensiveness and models self-compassion. If you need to revisit the conversation later, say, "I'm working on responding differently, but I slipped today. Thanks for your patience." Transparency encourages understanding, not judgment.

Your internal self-talk matters, too. Your inner critic may say, "You'll never change," but instead, acknowledge the slip with kindness: "Yeah, I slipped up, everyone does sometimes. That doesn't erase my progress." Talk to yourself the way you'd comfort a friend: "It was a tough moment. Tomorrow's another chance." Self-compassion isn't an excuse, but a way to sustain your efforts.

Support is essential, especially when old habits feel hard to shake. Build a "support toolkit" by identifying one or two people who understand your goals, maybe a friend building their own EQ skills, a supportive colleague, or your partner. Let them know you may reach out during challenging moments.

Support can also come from outside your immediate circle. Consider joining or starting an EQ accountability group, online or at work, or check in regularly with like-minded friends. Even a quick message like, "Today was tough, trying again tomorrow," helps keep you connected.

If you don't want to talk, use other supports. Revisit podcasts, videos, articles, or affirmations that encourage you. Keep them bookmarked or displayed ("Progress over perfection," "Pause before reacting," or "Keep going"). Some find music helps; a playlist for resets can soothe or energize you after a tough day.

Rituals also matter. Physical movement, even brief activities like walking, stretching, watering plants, or getting fresh air, can help shift stuck emotions more quickly than simply thinking alone.

If patterns persist, check for bigger issues. Assess whether you're overwhelmed, sleep-deprived, or stressed in other parts of life. Sometimes old habits reappear because your system is overloaded, not due to a lack of effort.

In these times, lower your expectations strategically. Instead of trying to change everything, focus on one small, manageable area. Let other parts of life run on autopilot so you can invest energy where it matters most.

Some days, nothing will work and everything will feel off. This is normal. Default to basic self-care: eat something nourishing, get outside, rest as much as possible, and try again tomorrow.

Reframe relapses as valuable feedback, not disasters. When old patterns return, treat them as clues about your triggers. Ask:

- What was different today?

- Did I skip my routine?

- Was I triggered by something new?

Use these insights to improve your approach; each mistake is valuable data.

Concrete reminders can help:

- Wear a bracelet to prompt a pause.

- Put sticky notes on your mirror.

- Set phone alarms with encouraging messages.

- Use a positive lock screen.

These small cues can nudge your brain toward better habits in stressful moments.

Rotate your supports as needed: some moments call for conversation, others for music, movement, or solitude. Over time, you'll learn what works best for different situations and struggles.

Every time you notice and adjust, even a little, you reinforce new, healthier patterns. Every attempt matters more than any setback. If others get frustrated with your ups and downs, let them know: "I'm working on this, I appreciate your patience." Most people value honesty and effort over flawless perfection.

Emotional growth isn't linear but moves in loops and zigzags. Old patterns will reappear some days, while newer ones come more easily on others. Progress means noticing sooner and recovering faster, not avoiding errors altogether.

With patience and practice, you'll catch old habits earlier and shift more smoothly. Your support toolkit will become more personalized and effective. Each time you choose a new response, even in small ways, you reinforce the habits that serve your present self better than those outdated reflexes ever did.

Celebrating Wins and Sustaining Growth With Progress Tracking

Building emotional intelligence often results in subtle changes, making it easy to overlook progress. That's why tracking growth is essential. Small victories, like remaining calm during conflict or responding kindly when tired, add up and deserve recognition. But since emotional growth can feel invisible, a mix of self-reflection, honest feedback, and creativity is key to keeping tabs on it.

Regular check-ins help keep you on track.

Try a monthly self-quiz with direct questions:

- How often did I pause before reacting?

- Did I express my feelings instead of bottling them up?

- Did I set boundaries or show empathy when it was hard?

Note your answers in a notebook, a digital note, or even a voice memo; the format matters less than your willingness to be honest.

Your own view can sometimes be skewed by emotion or self-doubt, so gather feedback from others you trust. Ask someone who's seen you in different situations if they've noticed any changes: "Did I handle stress differently?" or "Was I more open when we disagreed?" After a specific situation, ask for input on your response. These conversations may feel awkward, but they provide valuable insights you might miss.

Documenting your journey creatively can strengthen your motivation. Keep an EQ journal, writing a few lines each week about what worked, what didn't, and how you felt, to spot trends more easily. If you prefer structure or tech, use habit trackers or apps to log daily actions like active listening, expressing gratitude, or keeping calm under pressure. These can be visual, such as check marks, graphs, stickers, or colorful pens, to make progress tangible and enjoyable.

Celebrating wins, even small ones, keeps you engaged and reinforces positive change. After handling a conversation with extra patience, reward yourself: enjoy a treat, a walk, or time on a favorite hobby. Some like sharing milestones in group chats or on social media, and acknowledging progress also inspires others. If public sharing isn't your thing, confide in a friend who understands and supports your goals. Over time, these small celebrations become rituals that help new habits stick.

Sustaining growth requires ongoing attention. Set time aside each month to reflect: What challenged me? Where did I surprise myself? Which strategies worked best and which need tweaking? Use either formal worksheets with prompts ("Describe a situation handled differently" or "What new emotional skill did I practice?") or open-ended journaling to encourage self-awareness and consolidate learning.

For data lovers, mood-tracking apps reveal long-term patterns. Tag emotions and situations to spot trends, maybe Sunday evenings spike your stress, or certain people trigger old habits. These insights point to where to focus next.

To keep things fresh, periodically reset your intentions. Every quarter, revisit your goals or redo your initial 30-day challenge with adjustments based on what you've learned. You could focus on empathy one month, assertiveness the next, then stress regulation. Rotating focus keeps your EQ skills sharp.

Involving others helps too. Peer support circles, formal or informal, offer accountability, social connection, and motivation. Regularly meet with others practicing similar skills to share strategies and celebrate wins. This creates a supportive community where struggles and progress are both normalized.

Annual intentions also give structure to long-term growth. Each year or birthday, set one or two concrete EQ goals, such as handling feedback conversations better or deepening honesty with family. Keep these intentions visible and check in every few months, adjusting as needed. Don't judge yourself if things stall; growth isn't linear, and maintenance is sometimes enough.

Tie your EQ tracking to established routines for consistency; for example, reflect every Sunday evening or check your EQ tracker on payday alongside budgeting. Pairing reflection with regular habits helps make it stick.

When motivation dips, introduce fresh rewards or mini-challenges: read a new communication book, watch a documentary on relationships, or take a workshop. Minor adjustments can re-energize your commitment and prevent the process from becoming a chore.

Eventually, check-ins and celebrations become habits. You start noticing what goes right as much as what needs work, whether it's pausing before making a sarcastic remark, giving space for someone's feelings, or choosing gentle honesty over appeasement.

The goal isn't perfection, but resilience and flexibility. Setbacks happen, but with regular tracking and celebration, you'll recover faster and keep growing. New habits become natural, and emotional intelligence shows up everywhere, in how you talk to loved ones, manage workplace conflict, or treat yourself in tough times. These small changes ripple outward, making relationships and groups smoother, friendlier, and more fulfilling.

Sample Monthly EQ Reflection Worksheet

Here's a worksheet to structure your review:

- This month's biggest emotional win: _____

- A recurring challenge I noticed: _____

- What helped me stay calm or empathetic: _____

- One thing I'd like to try differently next month: _____

- Feedback I received from others (if any): _____

- My favorite way to celebrate my progress was: _____

Keep each month's sheet together so you can look back and notice clear patterns and improvements, as well as where minor tweaks could make a significant difference.

Tracking your progress makes emotional intelligence practical and lasting. Measuring growth, celebrating wins (big and small), and setting new intentions keep you moving forward even when motivation wanes. Next, we'll explore how these EQ skills can spur collective growth, helping teams, families, and communities reach their goals with more understanding and connection.

Conclusion

T ake a breath. Seriously, pause for a second. You made it, all the way to the end of this book, which is no small thing. If you're here, it means you care about showing up for yourself and for the people around you, even when things get messy. That's the heart of emotional intelligence, and honestly, it's the heart of everything that matters.

Let's bring it all together. From chapter one, I promised that you'd walk away with tools to communicate with empathy, collaborate with understanding, and actually reach your goals (both at home, with friends, and at work) without the usual frustration or endless misunderstandings. You've done the heavy lifting by reading, reflecting, and trying a few scripts or exercises. That's already a huge win.

Here's a quick recap, so it all sticks. First, we took EQ out of the clouds and made it real, demystifying what it is (and what it isn't). We talked about self-awareness, learning to spot your emotional triggers and name what you're feeling instead of bottling it up or letting it explode. Then we tackled self-regulation, how to pause, breathe, and choose your next move, even when your heart is pounding or your patience is thin. You practiced expressing tough feelings in honest, blame-free ways. You saw how empathy can actually bridge those sticky gaps between people.

We delved into the nuts and bolts of healthy communication, including active listening, giving feedback that lands, de-escalating tension, and making space for genuine repair when things go awry. You learned the power of boundaries, how to say "no" without guilt, protect your energy, and keep old family patterns from running the show. We talked about surviving stress, change, and those curveballs life throws, so you bounce back instead of burning out. Then we zoomed in on how EQ brings teams together at work, helping you speak up, read the (Zoom) room, and lead with integrity, whether you're the boss or just getting started. Finally, you picked up ways to make EQ a habit, using daily micro-actions, troubleshooting setbacks, and tracking your wins.

What does all this add up to? You now have a whole toolkit for navigating real life. You can notice when you're triggered and choose how to respond. You can talk about your feelings without drama or blame. You know how to set boundaries and protect your time, without endless apologies. You can bounce back from setbacks and even use those rough patches as fuel for growth. Most importantly, you can show up for your people, at home, at work, and everywhere in between, with more ease and a lot less stress.

And I want to pause here to say: I see the courage it takes. None of this is easy. Trying a new script, pausing when you want to snap, or setting a long overdue boundary takes guts. Maybe you stumbled, or felt awkward, or got pushback. That's normal. Every attempt counts, and every tiny shift is real progress. Suppose you journaled once, practiced active listening, or just named a feeling out loud. In that case, you're already changing the game, for yourself and everyone around you.

Maybe you still worry that you'll slip back into old habits. Spoiler: you will, sometimes. We all do. Emotional intelligence isn't a finish line you cross. It's more like tending a garden; sometimes things bloom, sometimes they wilt, but you keep showing up. Progress is messy. Perfection is not required. What matters is that you notice, pause, and try again. That's how resilience grows, and it's okay to have setbacks along the way.

So what now? Don't let this book gather dust. Go back to the exercises that hit home. Revisit the 30-Day EQ Challenge or use the troubleshooting guide the next time old patterns creep in. Keep tracking your growth, even if it's just a sticky note on the fridge or a quick check-in with a friend. And don't forget to revisit this book from time to time. Each time you do, you'll find new insights and new ways to apply the skills you've learned. These small habits, repeated, build real change over time.

And please, don't try to do it all alone. Share what you're learning. Find an accountability buddy, a group chat, or an online community where you can talk about your wins and your struggles. Model these skills for your family, your friends, and your coworkers. When you show up with empathy and honesty, you give everyone else permission to do the same. That's how real change spreads, one honest conversation, one boundary, one kind pause at a time. You're not alone in this journey.

Here's my simple challenge for you: pick one EQ skill from this book and try it today. It could be pausing before you react, setting a clear boundary at work, or offering extra empathy in a tough conversation. Don't wait for the "perfect" moment to start. Growth happens in the small, everyday choices. Those are the moments that add up. And remember, it's not just about trying it once, but about making it a regular part of your life. Regular practice is the key to mastering these skills.

Finally, thank you, from the bottom of my heart, for trusting me as your guide. I wrote this book because everyone (especially women, who so often carry the weight of emotional labor) deserves tools that actually work, not just more theory. Your willingness to try, to reflect, and to keep going inspires me. I'm cheering you on every step of the way.

So celebrate your progress, no matter how tiny it feels. Stay curious, keep practicing, and give yourself credit for every small win. You're building a foundation that will support you and everyone you care about for years to come. Let's keep moving forward, together, with a little more kindness, a little more courage, and a lot more connection.

More people may also benefit from the information in this book. However, they need your help to do so. If you found this book worthwhile and informative, please leave an honest review to help others recognize the value of this resource.

Thank you,
George Munson

Glossary

- **Active Listening:** Fully focusing on and understanding the speaker, "Active listening helped resolve our conflict."

- **Boundaries:** Personal limits to protect emotional well-being, "Setting boundaries with my team was a game changer."

- **Check-In:** A brief, intentional self- or group reflection, "Let's do a quick check-in before we start."

- **Emotional Agility:** Flexibility in dealing with emotions, "Emotional agility lets me adapt without losing myself."

- **Empathy Gap:** Difficulty understanding others' feelings, "There's an empathy gap between managers and staff."

- **EQ (Emotional Quotient):** Shorthand for emotional intelligence; often used in work and personal growth circles.

- **Feedback Loop:** Receiving and acting on input, "Creating a feedback loop made my team stronger."

- **Growth Mindset:** Believing you can develop abilities with effort, "I'm adopting a growth mindset around feedback."

- **Holding Space:** Creating a safe, nonjudgmental environment, "I need someone to hold space while I vent."

- **Mindful Pause:** Taking a moment to reflect before reacting, "A mindful pause keeps me from saying something I'll regret."

- **Resilience:** The capacity to recover from difficulties, "Building resilience has helped me handle setbacks."

- **Self-Compassion:** Treating yourself with kindness, "I'm practicing self-compassion when I mess up."

- **Self-Regulation:** The ability to manage one's own emotions, "I'm working on my self-regulation when I get stressed."

- **Show Up:** Being present and authentic, "I want to show up for my family, even on tough days."

- **Triggers:** Emotional cues or events that spark strong reactions, "That meeting was a trigger for me."

References

- *12 tips to tame stress.* (n.d.). Mayo Clinic. https://www.mayoclinic.org/healthy-lifestyle/stress-management/in-depth/stress-relievers/art-20047257

- 16Personalities, C. F. (2024, July 1). A 30-Day challenge to boost your emotional intelligence. *Leadership by 16Personalities.* https://16personalities.substack.com/p/30-day-challenge-emotional-intelligence

- Arocho, J., PhD, & Arocho, J., PhD. (2024, July 2). *Assertive vs. Aggressive: What's the Difference? - Manhattan CBT.* Manhattan Center for Cognitive Behavioral Therapy. https://manhattancbt.com/assertive-vs-aggressive/

- Cuncic, A., MA. (2024, February 12). *7 Active listening techniques for better communication.* Verywell Mind. https://www.verywellmind.com/what-is-active-listening-3024343

- Els, L. C. (2024, August 8). *Self-regulation for adults: Strategies for getting a handle on emotions and behavior.* Harvard Health. https://www.health.harvard.edu/mind-and-mood/self-regulation-for-adults-strategies-for-getting-a-handle-on-emotions-and-behavior

- Expert, C. (2025, July 7). *32 Phrases to help you express Empathy.*

The Conflict Expert. https://the-conflictexpert.com/2019/08/06/32-phrases-to-help-you-express-empathy/

- *Express your needs | The Personal Development School.* (n.d.). Personal Development School. https://university.personaldevelopmentschool.com/courses/expressing-your-needs-scripts-for-effective-communication

- *Feelings wheel.* (n.d.). https://feelingswheel.com/

- Gallo, A. (2023, February 15). *What is psychological safety?* Harvard Business Review. https://hbr.org/2023/02/what-is-psychological-safety

- Grecucci, A., Pappaianni, E., Siugzdaite, R., Theuninck, A., & Job, R. (2015). Mindful Emotion Regulation: Exploring the Neurocognitive Mechanisms behind Mindfulness. *BioMed Research International, 2015*, 1–9. https://doi.org/10.1155/2015/670724

- Hayley. (2025, September 19). *How to set boundaries at work – with examples.* https://halopsychology.com/2024/11/12/how-to-set-boundaries-at-work-with-examples/

- Hinton, A. O., McReynolds, M. R., Martinez, D., Shuler, H. D., & Termini, C. M. (2020). The power of saying no. *EMBO Reports, 21*(7). https://doi.org/10.15252/embr.202050918

- Hitchcock, S. (2023, October 5). *Objective feedback made easier - the SBIR method.* https://www.linkedin.com/pulse/objective-feedback-made-easier-sbir-method-scott-hitchcock

- Hollingsworth, J. C., & Redden, D. T. (2022). Tiny Habits® for Gratitude-Implications for healthcare education stakeholders. *Frontiers in Public Health, 10.* https://doi.org/10.3389/fpubh.2022.866992

- *How stress affects your body and behavior.* (n.d.). Mayo Clinic. https://www.mayoclinic.org/healthy-lifestyle/stress-management/in-depth/stress-symptoms/art-20050987

- Lee, J. (2019, October 2). *Scripts for responding to negative f e e d b a c k .* https://www.linkedin.com/pulse/scripts-responding-negative-feedback-jamie-lee

- Lim, M. D., & Lau, M. C. (2021). Can we "Brain-Train" Emotional intelligence? A narrative review on the features and approaches used in ability EI training studies. *Frontiers in Psychology, 12.* https://doi.org/10.3389/fpsyg.2021.569749

- Lmft, J. K. (2019, October 29). A crucial tool for life coaching and relationships. *Psychology Today.* https://www.psychologytoday.com/us/blog/the-angry-therapist/201910/what-does-it-meanlook-hold-space-someone

- Ma, F., Wylie, B. E., Luo, X., He, Z., Jiang, R., Zhang, Y., Xu, F., & Evans, A. D. (2019). Apologies repair trust via perceived trustworthiness and negative emotions. *Frontiers in Psychology, 10.* https://doi.org/10.3389/fpsyg.2019.00758

- Mansuri, A. (2024, December 18). *Stress vs. Burnout: What's the Difference?* Healthline. https://www.healthline.com/health/stress-vs-burnout

- Marc Brackett. (2024, November 3). *How we feel app - Marc Brackett Emotional Intelligence Tool.* https://marcbrackett.com/how-we-feel-app-3/

- Melody. (2025, July 6). Speak confidently in work meetings (Even when anxious). *Melody Wilding.*

https://melodywilding.com/speak-confidently-meetings-when-anxious/

- Messier, S. (2018, March 8). *Giving feedback? Try the SBIR framework*. https://www.linkedin.com/pulse/giving-feedback-try-sbir-framework-stacey-messier

- *MindTools | Home*. (n.d.). https://www.mindtools.com/an0fzpz/the-grow-model-of-coaching-and-mentoring

- MSEd, K. C. (2023, December 31). *5 key emotional intelligence skills*. Verywell Mind. https://www.verywellmind.com/components-of-emotional-intelligence-2795438

- Pollack, J. (2025, May 9). 9 Examples of De-Escalation situations in diverse industries | Pollack Peacebuilding Systems. *Pollack Peacebuilding Systems*. https://pollackpeacebuilding.com/blog/examples-of-de-escalation/

- *Preventing and Managing Team Conflict - Professional & Executive Development | Harvard DCE*. (2024, January 8). Professional & Executive Development | Harvard DCE. https://professional.dce.harvard.edu/blog/preventing-and-managing-team-conflict/

- Price, N. (2023, December 12). *Author Post: Empathy is important, and so are boundaries*. Forbes. https://www.forbes.com/sites/forbesbooksauthors/2023/12/12/empathy-is-important-and-so-are-boundaries/

- Rogers, S. L., Howieson, J., & Neame, C. (2018). I understand you feel that way, but I feel this way: the benefits of I-language and communicating perspective during conflict. *PeerJ*, *6*, e4831. https://doi.org/10.7717/peerj.4831

- *Safety Plan - Emotional Safety Planning - The hotline.* (2021, November 2). The Hotline. https://www.thehotline.org/resources/emotional-safety-planning/

- Valera, S. (2024, October 25). *Best Mood Tracker Apps.* Verywell M i n d . https://www.verywellmind.com/best-mood-tracker-apps-5212922

- Wadmin, Wadmin, & Wadmin. (2025, February 19). *Find your personal triggers in 7 simple steps and strengthen your mental health.* Mindful Health Solutions -. https://mindfulhealthsolutions.com/find-your-personal-triggers-in-7-simple-steps/

- Wilson, J. (2025, February 21). 8 "Micro-Habits" that can help you live a happier, healthier life. *HuffPost.* https://www.huffpost.com/entry/micro-habits-benefits_l_67aa0d0ce4b0ade4a9a34ed5

www.ingramcontent.com/pod-product-compliance
Lightning Source LLC
Chambersburg PA
CBHW060046150626
46556CB00018BA/2905